全国高等学校外语教师丛书·讲

王艳 著

英语听力课堂
活动设计

Designing Classroom Activities
for English Listening

外语教学与研究出版社
FOREIGN LANGUAGE TEACHING AND RESEARCH PRESS
北京 BEIJING

图书在版编目（CIP）数据

英语听力课堂活动设计 / 王艳著. –– 北京 ：外语教学与研究出版社，2022.8
（2025.8 重印）
（全国高等学校外语教师丛书. 课堂活动系列）
ISBN 978-7-5213-3931-4

I.①英… II.①王… III.①英语－听说教学－教学研究－高等学校 IV.①H319.9

中国版本图书馆 CIP 数据核字 (2022) 第 153927 号

出 版 人　王　芳
项目负责　段长城
责任编辑　都帮森
责任校对　陈　阳
封面设计　覃一彪
版式设计　吴德胜
出版发行　外语教学与研究出版社
社　　址　北京市西三环北路 19 号（100089）
网　　址　https://www.fltrp.com
印　　刷　北京九州迅驰传媒文化有限公司
开　　本　650×980　1/16
印　　张　11.5
版　　次　2022 年 10 月第 1 版 2025 年 8 月第 7 次印刷
书　　号　ISBN 978-7-5213-3931-4
定　　价　46.90 元

如有图书采购需求，图书内容或印刷装订等问题，侵权、盗版书籍等线索，请拨打以下电话或关注官方服务号：
客服电话：400 898 7008
官方服务号：微信搜索并关注公众号"外研社官方服务号"
外研社购书网址：https://fltrp.tmall.com

物料号：339310001

记载人类文明
沟通世界文化
www.fltrp.com

目　录

总　序

　　"全国高等学校外语教师丛书"是外语教学与研究出版社高等英语教育出版分社近期精心策划、隆重推出的系列丛书，包含理论指导、科研方法和教学研究三个子系列。本套丛书既包括学界专家精心挑选的国外引进著作，又有特邀国内学者执笔完成的"命题作文"。作为开放的系列丛书，该丛书还将根据外语教学与科研的发展不断增加新的专题，以便教师研修与提高。

　　编者有幸参与了这套系列丛书的策划工作。在策划过程中，我们分析了高校英语教师面临的困难与挑战，考察了一线教师的需求，最终确立这套丛书选题的指导思想为：想外语教师所想，急外语教师所急，顺应广大教师的发展需求；确立这套丛书的写作特色为：突出科学性、可读性和操作性，做到举重若轻，条理清晰，例证丰富，深入浅出。

　　第一个子系列是"理论指导"。该系列力图为教师提供某学科或某领域的研究概貌，期盼读者能用较短的时间了解某领域的核心知识点与前沿研究课题。以《二语习得重点问题研究》一书为例，该书不求面面俱到，只求抓住二语习得研究领域中的热点、要点和富有争议的问题，动态展开叙述。每一章的写作以不同意见的争辩为出发点，对取向相左的理论、实证研究结果差异进行分析、梳理和评述，最后介绍或者展望国内外的最新发展趋势。全书阐述清晰，深入浅出，易读易懂。再比如《认知语言学与二语教学》一书，全书分为理论篇、教学篇与研究篇三个部分。理论篇阐述认知语言学视角下的语言观、教学观与学习观，以及与二语教学相关的认知语言学中的主要概念与理论；教学篇选用认知语言学领域比较成熟的理论，探讨应用到中国英语教学实践的可能性；研究篇包括国内外将认知语言学理论应用到教学实践中的研究综述、研究方法介绍以及对未来研究的展望。

　　第二个子系列是"科研方法"。该系列介绍了多种研究方法，通常是一本书介绍一种方法，例如问卷调查、个案研究、行动研究、有声思维、语料库研究、微变化研究和启动研究等。也有的书涉及多种方法，综合描述量化研究或者质化研究，例如：《应用语言学中的质性研究与分析》、《应用语言学中的量化研究与分析》和《第二语言研究中的数据收集方法》等。凡入选本系列丛书的著作人，无论是国外著者还是国内著者，均有高度的读者意识，乐于为一线教师开展教学科研服务，力求做到帮助读者"排忧解难"。例如，澳大利亚安妮·伯恩斯（Anne Burns）教授撰写的《英语教学中的行动研究方法》一书，从一线教师的视角，讨论行动研究的各个环节，每章均有"反思时刻"、"行动时刻"等新颖形式设计。同时，全书运用了丰富例证来解释理论概念，便于读者理解、思考和消化所读内容。凡是应邀撰写研究方法系列的中国著作人均有博士学位，并对自己阐述的研究方法有着丰富的实践经验。他们有的运用了书中的研究方法完成了硕士、博士论文，有的采用书中的研究方法从事过重大科研项目。以秦晓晴教授撰写的《外语教学问卷调查法》一书为例，该书著者将系统性与实用性有机结合，根据实施问卷调查法的流程，系统地介绍了问卷调查研究中问题的提出、问卷项目设计、问卷试测、问卷实施、问卷整理及数据准备、问卷评价以及问卷数据汇总及统计分析方法选择等环节。书中各个环节的描述都配有易于理解的研究实例。

第三个子系列是"教学研究"。该系列与前两个系列相比，有两点显著不同：第一，本系列侧重同步培养教师的教学能力与教学研究能力；第二，本系列所有著作的撰稿人主要为中国学者。有些著者虽然目前在海外工作和生活，但他们出国前曾在国内高校任教，也经常回国参与国内的教学与研究工作。本系列包括《英语听力教学与研究》、《英语写作教学与研究》、《英语阅读教学与研究》、《英语口语教学与研究》、《翻译教学与研究》等。以《英语听力教学与研究》一书为例，著者王艳副教授拥有十多年的听力教学经验，同时听力教学研究又是她博士论文的选题领域。《英语听力教学与研究》一书，浓缩了她多年来听力教学与听力教学研究的宝贵经验。全书分为两部分：教学篇与研究篇。教学篇中涉及了听力教学的各个重要环节以及学生在听力学习中可能碰到的困难与应对的办法，所选用的案例均来自著者课堂教学的真实活动。研究篇中既有著者的听力教学研究案例，也有著者从国内外文献中筛选出的符合中国国情的听力教学研究案例，综合在一起加以分析阐述。

　　第四个子系列是"课堂活动"。该系列汇集了各分册作者多年来的一线教学经验，旨在为教师提供具体、真实、具有较高借鉴价值的课堂活动案例，提高教师的课堂教学能力。该系列图书包括《英语阅读教学活动设计》《英语听力课堂活动设计》《英语合作式学习活动》等。以《英语阅读教学活动设计》一书为例，阅读教学是学生学习语言知识和教师培养学生思维的重要途径和载体。该书第一作者陈则航教授多年来致力于英语阅读教学研究，希望通过该书与读者分享如何进行具体的阅读教学活动设计，探讨如何在课堂教学中落实阅读教学理念。该书包括三个部分。第一部分介绍在阅读前、阅读中和阅读后这三个不同阶段教师可以设计的阅读教学活动，并且介绍了阅读测评的目的、原则和方式。第二部分探讨了如何通过阅读教学促进学生思维发展。第三部分展示了教师在阅读课堂中的真实教学案例，并对其进行了分析与点评，以期为改进阅读教学活动设计提供启示。

　　教育大计，教师为本。"全国高等学校外语教师丛书"内容全面，出版及时，必将成为高校教师提升自我教学能力、研究能力与合作能力的良师益友。编者相信本套丛书的出版对高校外语教师个人专业能力的提高，对教师队伍整体素质的提高，必将起到积极的推动作用。

文秋芳

北京外国语大学中国外语与教育研究中心

2011 年 7 月 3 日

前　言

2013 年暑假，外语教学与研究出版社在长沙举办了一次教学研讨会。在会上，我很荣幸作为讲座人，和来自全国各地的老师们探讨外语听力教学。在与参会教师们交流互动的环节中，我收到很多老师递过来的小纸条，上面写着他们在听力教学中遇到的一些问题。有一位老师写道："听力课上，学生往往学得很被动。他们被动地去听和理解信息，缺乏动力和兴趣，而且由于心理因素的影响，在练习过程中气氛紧张，效果不佳。如何将学生的学习主动性、听力学习规律与课堂设计结合起来，达到一个生动有效的效果，这是一直困惑我的问题。"

这位老师的问题很有代表性。听力教学面临的共性问题包括学生积极性不高、教学目标不明确、课堂教学形式单一、教师缺乏指导学生提高水平的方法，等等。在交流中还发现，听力课教师认可听力教学的重要性，但对听力教学的复杂性认识不够。他们希望上好听力课，让学生提高水平，但是对如何达成这个目标充满困惑。许多老师希望我介绍一些听力活动，他们可以拿去就用。可以看出，他们迫切希望找到能提高课堂教学有效性的方法。我推荐了自己刚刚出版的《英语听力教学与研究》。我在这本书的教学篇中，设计了从语音、词汇、语法、语篇和策略能力等五方面入手提高听力技能的教学活动。同时，我也在思考如何全面拓展。

长沙研讨会之后的几年中，我国高等教育进一步深化改革，旨在切实提高人才培养质量，推进内涵式发展。这期间，我受外研社邀请，加入北京外国语大学思辨英语系列教材的编写团队，主编《大学思辨英语教程视听说》1—4册。在编写过程中，我切身体会到，随着我国国力的增强和国际地位的提高，国家和社会对外语人才的培养提出了更高的要求。传统的外语听力课堂应加快改革，不断开拓创新，从而提高人才培养质量，全面提升学生的素质、知识和能力。

在长沙研讨会上收到的这些纸条，我保留至今。近年来，我又多次参加听力教学研讨活动，收集了更多学生和教师的反馈。我把与他们的交流同自己教学实践中的心得以及科研中的探索放在一起，写成这本新作。在书中，我以听力目的为视角，从理解、思辨、跨文化、学术和欣赏等五个目标探讨听力课堂活动的设计，期望能为教师在提高学生语言能力、思辨能力、跨文化能力、学科知识和人文素养等方面助一臂之力。

我首先要特别感谢孙有中教授及北外思辨英语系列教材编写团队的所有老师，引领我踏入思辨和跨文化领域，拓展了听力教学中能力培养的空间。没有你们的启发，我不会发现这一片新天地。感谢外研社的编辑陈阳老师和李晓雨老师，感谢你们耐心的等待，也让我有机会不断把最新的思考纳入书中。责任编辑都帮森老师对全书进行了细致和专业的审校，我在此特别致谢。在这本书写作期间，我正在编写《大学思辨英语教程视听说》，本书的一些素材来自这套教材，感谢外研社高英分社的伙伴们一如既往的支持和帮助。感谢我的导师文秋芳教授和丁言仁教授，在我教学和科研的道路上给予的关心和指导，让我时刻谨记教学研究的重要性。最后，感谢我的家人，是你们付出了时间，换来我能有时间写作。本书是我个人的实践心得，并不试图要给出一个完美的方案，书中不当之处，恳请广大读者批评指正。

王艳

南京大学

2022 年 4 月 6 日

第一章 绪论

本章作为全书的开篇，旨在帮助广大读者了解本书的写作目的、内容结构和使用方法。本章将首先简要介绍听力的本质，以帮助读者了解听力教学的复杂性，然后阐述本书以"学"为中心展开课堂活动设计的理念，最后介绍本书的使用方法。

1.1 为什么要写听力课堂活动设计？

听力在外语学习中占有举足轻重的地位。听是外语交流的前提和基础，它不仅决定外语交流的顺畅程度，还影响外语学习者语言能力的整体发展。在世界各国的交往越来越广泛和深入的今天，良好的外语听说能力已经成为人才培养之必备。然而，由于种种原因，听力教学与研究长期以来一直被忽视（Vandergrift & Goh 2012）。这与听力本身的复杂性有一定的关系。

与读和写相比，听是对口头语言的处理。与对书面文字的处理不同的是，听具有在线性和即时性的特点。在阅读和写作过程中，看不懂可以多看几遍，写不出来也有时间反复思考，学习者在一定程度上可以自主支配时间。但是，听的过程要求听者即时理解，没有机会多次回顾。在真实的交流中，如果听不懂，也不可能让说话人多次重复。与说相比，听是接受，说是产出。在说的时候，不会说的可以不说，或者换一种方式说，但是在听的过程中，听者不能决定所听的内容，也不能决定说话人的语速和口音，等等。因此，从本质上说，听懂一门外语并不容易。

Rost（2011）从神经科学、语言学、语义学和语用学等四个维度对听进行了定义。第一，听是人的生理机能。在听的时候，人的神经系统参与工作，产生意识、施加注意力。注意力具有有限性和选择性两个特点。人的大脑一次只能处理一个信息源，尽管我们可以在不同信息源之间来回切换，或者把它们集中起来一并处理。正因为注意力资源的有限性，当大脑面对众多信息源时，必须做出选择（Rost 2011：20）。选择性注意是听力过程的一个重要特点，因为没有被注意到的，自然就得不到处理，也就谈不上理解或者习得。

第二，从语言学角度来看，听涉及一系列解码过程，如语音信号的感知、词汇的识别、音位结构规则的使用、语法解析，以及韵律特征和非语言线索的利用，等等。大脑中关于语言的各种知识也被运用在听力理解过程中。这种"自下而上"的处理过程（由所听的语言信号驱动）和"自上而下"（由大脑中的概念驱动）的处理过程是并行和互补的，它们相互协同，完成对语言的理解（Rost 2011：52）。

第三，从语义学层面来讲，听要实现对说话人话语的理解，即听者理解所听语言在个人体验或客观世界中的所指。这涉及听者和说话人的知识结构，心理学家称之为图式。图式正是听者在理解口头语言时所不可缺少的。听的时候，相关的图式被激活，随时供大脑调用。同时，听者能在多大程度上理解说话人的意思，还取决于两人共同拥有的对这个世界的知识和看法。因此，听的过程既是一个认知被调动的过程，也是一个社会因素在起作用的过程。对于理解过程中遇到的缺失或者没有明说的信息，听者会采用自己的知识去推断说话人的意思。因此，听的过程是形成假设和验证假设的过程，也是决策的过程（Rost 2011：57）。然而，即便如此忙碌，大脑仍然可能错过某些词和句子，或者来不及决策。这时，听者会使用策略来弥补。因此，在听的过程中，听者实际上非但不是被动在听，反而是在主动参与。

第四，从语用学层面看，听不仅仅是指语言的感知、解码和语义处理，还包括应听出真正的含义。说话人和听者都有会话意图。在交流中，他们不断指向时间、地点、事件、人物、物体、状态等，交流双方通过互动促成会话的意义。从听者的角度来看，如果不关注这些要素，那么即便没有语言的困难，也可能在理解上有偏差。理解说话人的意图，也应成为听的首要目标（Rost 2011：78）。

由此可见，听的过程极为复杂，听懂外语并不是一项容易掌握的技能。事实上，听力仍然是外语基础技能教学中的薄弱环节，听力也仍然被许多学生认为是最难提高的能力。那么，怎样才能让听力课堂成为有效提高听力的地方？

1.2　课堂活动设计是什么？

　　美国教育学家泰勒（R. Tyler）1949 年在《课程与教学的基本原理》一书中提到课程设计的四条基本原则，即：1）明确合适的学习目标；2）确定有用的学习经验；3）组织学习经验使教学更有效；4）评估课程并改进被证明无效的做法。用现在的术语来表述，这四条原则分别指的是教学目标、教学内容、教学组织和教学评估。课堂活动设计属于如何组织教学的范畴，解决的是怎样上课的问题，但它与其他三条原则是相辅相成的。

　　课堂活动设计与课程质量紧密相关。课程是人才培养的核心要素，是"教"和"学"发生的载体和场所。要创建具有高阶性、创新性和挑战度的优质课程，必须重视和加强课堂设计。传统的听力课堂大多以"理解法"为主要方式（Field 2008），教师播放听力材料，学生做听力练习题。听完之后，教师核对答案。这种"放录音、对答案"的方法更像是在测试，难免枯燥乏味。对一部分听力困难大的学生来说，焦虑感也比较高。当然，它的最大弊端还在于无法从根本上发现学生听力问题的根源，从而不能有针对性地采取办法来帮助学生解决这些问题。学生一方面觉得自己听力困难很多，一方面却对听力课提不起兴趣，直到课程结束，也仍然感到自己的能力没有得到提高。有效的听力课堂应该将上述的四条原则紧密结合，首先根据大纲和标准制定明确的教学目标，然后分析达成目标的途径并制定具体的方案，再选择合适的材料、运用合适的课堂活动来实现。在实施过程中，应充分了解学习者知识、态度、水平的变化，动态评估教学效果。因此，本书并不只是单个活动设计的集合，而是力求遵循上述这些原则，在充分阐述教学目标和教学方案的基础上，再以案例说明课堂活动的设计。

　　众所周知，我国的课堂教学理念正在实现从以教师"教"为中心到以学生"学"为中心的转变。以"学"为中心的课堂是以学生的学习活动为教学核心，以学生的全人发展为本。在以"教"为中心的课堂上，教师传递知识，只需要 chalk 和 talk，学生则是被动接受的角色。前面说到的听力教学"理解法"则与以"教"为中心的方法是一脉相承的。而以"学"为中心的教学理念，则以学生为认知主体，认为知识是学生主动建构的，而不是教师灌输的。在这种理念下，教学设计的核心是激发学生主动建构知识，并为此创设必要的情境。"学习是活动，活动获得经验，经验改变大脑"（赵炬明 2018）。在交流、合作、互动和探究中，学生的素质、知识和能力得到全面发展。这同样也是听力课堂活动设计所应遵循的理念。

1.3 本书的内容和结构

怎样才能设计好听力课堂活动？笔者认为，课堂活动设计应遵循明确的教学目标，考虑学生现有的水平、需求和发展阶段，解决学生疑难，促进有效学习的产生；应以国内外语言学领域，特别是听力领域的学术成果和教学经验为基础，体现活动的科学性、合理性和实用性；应紧密联系真实生活的情境，充分为学生提供合作互动的机会；应尽可能富有趣味和成效，让学生积极参与并学有所得。本书各章节的内容设计和结构安排遵循了这些理念。

1.3.1 能力目标导向

随着国际形势变化和我国国际地位提高，国家对于外语人才培养提出了更高要求（胡文仲 2018）。教育部高等学校教学指导委员会于 2018 年颁布了中国高等教育领域首个教学质量国家标准——《普通高等学校本科专业类教学质量国家标准》。其中的《外国语言文学类教学质量国家标准》（以下简称《国标》），对外语类专业学生的素质要求是"具有正确的世界观、人生观和价值观，良好的道德品质，中国情怀和国际视野，社会责任感，人文与科学素养，合作精神，创新精神以及学科基本素养"；知识要求包括"外国语言知识、外国文学知识、国别与区域知识，熟悉中国语言文化知识，了解相关专业知识以及人文社会科学与自然科学基础知识，形成跨学科知识结构，体现专业特色"；能力要求包括"具备外语运用能力、文学赏析能力、跨文化能力、思辨能力，以及一定的研究能力、创新能力、信息技术应用能力、自主学习能力和实践能力"。从《国标》可以看出，对外语专业学生的要求在提高，不仅要求外语技能，还要求具备人文素养、专业知识、思辨能力、跨文化能力和学术能力，等等。

对于大学外语教育，国家也提出了新的定位。《大学英语教学指南（2020版）》（以下简称《指南》）指出，大学英语兼具工具性和人文性。工具性重在提升语言应用能力，提升跨文化交际能力和思辨能力，增强运用英语进行专业和学术交流的能力；人文性表现在注重以人为本，注重学生的综合素质培养和全面发展。大学英语课程需在课程建设、教材编写、教学实施等各个环节努力实现工具性和人文性的统一（教育部高等学校大学外语教学指导委员会，2020：3）。可见，无论是专业外语教育还是大学外语教育，均要求人才培养更加全面、多元、融合，以满足时代和社会的需要。

在《国标》的规定中，听力课程或视听说课程在各外语专业中均为核心课。以英语为例，英语专业核心课程不再含有"英语听力"，而是改为"英语视听说"。为什么从"听力课"改为"视听说课"？主要有两点原因，一是20世纪80—90年代的听力课大都采用听音频的方式，而后来视频原声材料大量出现，丰富了输入模式，提高了语言真实度，输入方式变为"视"和"听"；二是为了重视"视""听""说"的结合，旨在综合提高语言运用能力。虽然名为"视听说"课程，但是要培养的核心能力还是"听"，不能忽视。"听"和"说"这两种能力，尽管两者之间有密切的联系，但从语言习得的本质上说相当不同。在二语研究领域，两者是分开研究的。而且，无论在国际考试系统还是国内语言能力标准中，"听"都是单独测试的技能，如《欧洲语言共同参考框架》和《中国英语能力等级量表》都把听力单列。"视听说"课所训练的核心技能"听"，正如"英语口语"课所训练的核心技能为"说"一样，两门课程各有其不同的聚焦。本书的目标是听力活动的设计，并不刻意突出"视"和"说"。这是因为，在听力课程中采用视频作为输入材料已经非常普遍，听前听后的练习也常常采用说的方式，"听力课程"与"视听说课程"在本质上并不矛盾，教学目标也是一致的。同样地，本书的活动设计常常融合听和说的活动，这也不影响教学专注实现听力能力的各个目标。

本书以发展语言能力、思辨能力、跨文化能力、学术能力，以及外语歌曲和影片赏析能力为目标来设计听力课堂活动。从第二到第六章，分别为理解型听力活动、思辨听力活动、跨文化听力活动、学术听力活动和欣赏型听力活动。

1.3.2　了解学生需求

　　好的活动设计离不开对学生需求的了解。学生的需求主要包括学生未来使用语言的目标、对这门课程的期待和自身的困难与不足。学生来到听力课堂，大都抱有远期和近期的目标。远期的目标可能是在将来工作中流畅使用外语，顺利通过四、八级考试，为出国留学做准备，等等；近期目标也许包括通过课程考试、拿到学分、能不借助字幕看懂原版影片，等等。教师清楚了解学生的需求，对设计活动十分有好处，比如可以在设置活动情境、选择材料的内容、话题和难度等方面做到有目的、有依据，从而增强活动的有用性和真实性。教师可以把学生个人需求与专业培养标准充分挂钩，使学生明确教学目标与个人需求的关系，从而更加积极主动地投入学习。

　　除了了解学生学习语言的目的，教师对学生的听力困难也应清楚掌握。学生所表述的困难，往往是对现象的描述，比如"语速太快，我听不懂"，表面上是语速的原因，而实际上可能是语音识别能力弱或者听力词汇量不足；又如"句子一长，我就跟不上了，听了后面忘了前面"，这表面上看是没有记住，但其实是因为学生没有理解所听到的信息或者理解不充分，导致所处理的信息还留在短时记忆中，被后来进入的信息挤掉的缘故。教师应能透过现象看本质，通过对听力困难的分析，发现学生的根本问题所在。

　　学生所表述的困难，还能反映出他们在听力活动中的行为、观念和态度。例如，常常听学生说"我能听懂一些词，但是来不及把所有的都翻译出来"，这表明该学生可能认为，听就应该听懂每一个词，而且还要翻译成中文来理解。其实这是一个误区。除了听写段落这种精听练习，学生不太需要在听的时候把注意力集中在每一个词上，而且这也很难做到。因为人的注意力是有限的，在听的过程中通常是选择性地施加注意，无法面面俱到。如果学生带着这种错误的观念去听，就可能导致策略使用出错，如纠结于某个细节，结果错过后面的重要内容，或者没有抓住主旨。把每个词都翻译过来再理解，导致理解路径变长，大脑很快就会来不及处理源源不断进来的信息。教师应通过耐心倾听学生对困难的表述，剖析其行为、观念和态度上的原因，准确发现其薄弱环节和不当策略使用，有的放矢地进行活动设计。

　　建构主义理论认为，学生的知识并不是教师传授的，而是自己建构的。教师的角色是创建适合的环境，搭建适合的脚手架，帮助学生学习。因此，只有了解学生的需求，教师才知道如何去帮助学生建构。因此，本书在每章开篇都会安排一个结合学生困难和教学困惑的小案例予以引入，在目标阐述和教学具体实例中也会涉及学生的常见听力困难。

1.3.3　运用听力研究成果

　　20 世纪 80 年代之前，听力技能并没有得到足够的研究。由于"听"的输入是声音信号，不像"读"有方便研究的文本，也不像"说"和"写"有方便研究的输出。听力研究本身的难度使听力教学的研究也一直滞后于其他技能教学的研究。直到 20 世纪 80 年代，情况才有所改变。人们认为把听力理解技能分解成微技能，逐个学习，就能提高听力水平。Richards（1983）提出 33 条听力微技能，包括区别单词重音、识别讲座主题、识别语篇标记、推断说话人关系，等等。这一列表的缺点是没有实证研究支撑，也没有按照认知难度排序（Aryadoust 2018）。后来的研究发现，二语学习者在听力测试中主要使用的微技能只包括理解关键词、理解明晰信息、理解细节等（Goh & Aryadoust 2015）。另一种常见的分法是宏观技能和微观技能，前者是指听者使用背景知识、概念结构等去构建图景，对应"自上而下"的处理方式；后者是指从感知发音到识别词汇、理解句子意思等一系列技能，对应"自下而上"的处理方式。

　　从 20 世纪 90 年代开始，对听力策略的研究出现。O'Malley & Chamot（1990）研究了听力过程中元认知策略、认知策略、社会-情感策略的使用，发现当实验组的学生主动施加注意、采用笔记策略和合作策略来完成听力任务时，表现好于对照组，虽然统计上并不显著。随后，Mendelsohn（1995）提出策略教学法，认为听力教学应旨在教会学生听的方法，通过了解语言功能，发展元认知意识和能力来完成听力任务。Thompson & Rubin（1996）证实了策略使用与听力表现有一定显著性的联系。Vandergrift 等（2006）开发了听力元认知意识问卷，旨在加强学习者对元认知策略的使用意识。随后，不少实证研究佐证了策略使用对语言学习和有效完成听力任务的积极作用（如 Graham &

Macaro 2008；Vandergrift & Tafaghodtari 2010）。以策略学习为目标的教学方法将听力过程由被动变为主动，使听力水平不那么高的学生有更多办法来处理交流中的障碍，以及应对测试。

20 世纪 90 年代中期，对互动听力的重视，加上视频材料的普及，促使视听说教学发展起来。互动听力是指双向听力，即在对话中交流，而不是像听新闻、听讲座这样的单向听力。单向聆听无法体现互动，而双向听力既可加强语篇理解，又能在交流中促进对话语真正含义的理解，还能够锻炼策略使用能力（Buck 1995）。此外，互动听力还可练习即时解码、思辨技能和"听—想—说"同时进行的复杂技能（Morley 1995）。在互动听力中，双方通过合作来争取让对方听懂，这一过程提供了意义协商的机会，能够促进语言的发展（Brown 1995）。上述这些研究，促使传统听力课向注重互动的视听说课程转变。

听力领域的研究成果对听力教学方法产生了直接的影响。虽然，随着时间的推移，教学的要求和条件也在发生改变，但是了解前人的研究方法和结论仍然十分重要，能为教学活动的设计提供经验和依据，从而扬长避短，力求做到中国语境下的创新。本书各章在撰写具体听力教学方案时，会对听力学术领域相应的研究做出回顾和引证。

1.3.4　综合听力教学经验与方法

Vandergrift & Goh（2012）在对第二语言听力教学法的回顾中，总结了不同历史时期的代表性方法，即注重文本理解、注重交流理解、注重学习者这三种教学方法。20 世纪 50—60 年代的听力教学深受读写教学法的影响，听力材料大都是书面文本的朗读录音，并不是生活中原汁原味的口头语言。书面文本的词汇和语法比口语复杂，听力过程中的认知负担相对较重。听力学习者需通过回答听力理解问题来检查自己是否听得正确，也就使课堂很像测试。这些题目有的是考查对全篇主旨的理解，有的是考查是否听懂了某个细节。这一教学法类似前面提到的"理解法"，直到现在还在很多听力课堂上使用。

20 世纪 70 年代之后，交际法出现。受其影响，听力课也将交际作为目的，听力输入采用原汁原味的听力材料，或是取自真实录音录像，或是模拟真实生活的场景。20 世纪 80 年代初风靡全国的英语教学节目《跟我学》(*Follow Me*) 采用的就是交际法。同时，借助听英文歌曲和看电影来学习英语的方法也开始兴起。这一阶段，听力被视为由很多微技能组成的复杂技能，所提倡的教学方法也以提高微技能为特点，如训练区分词汇边界、识别关键词、根据上下文猜测词汇含义、推断事件之间的联系，等等。微技能把听力细化，易于诊断学生的困难，易于操作。

20 世纪 90 年代左右兴起的对听力策略的研究，促使教学开始注重学习者意识和学习过程，注重教会学生怎么去听。教师通过培养学生的策略意识和策略使用能力，使他们能够更好地掌控听力过程。策略除了认知策略和情感策略外，还包括用来管理认知的元认知策略。这种方法强调学生对自身学习进行反思，通过内省式和基于过程的学习活动来提高听力。这种方法有助于学习者增强自我调控学习过程的意识和能力，从而使他们在课外以及离开学校后，都知道如何继续学习。

除了 Vandergrift & Goh（2012）所概述的这三种教学方法，合作听力作为一种新兴的方法，正在受到重视。在听力课堂上，学习者组成对子或小组，他们的互动能否促进对听力材料的理解和听力能力的发展，引起了研究者的广泛兴趣。Cross（2010）和 Vandergrift & Goh（2012）认为，同伴之间的讨论能够激活和调节学习者计划、监控、评价和解决问题的过程，让他们对作为二语学习者的自己更加了解，对听力任务的性质、需求以及听力策略的使用等也更加清楚。笔者也通过一项研究发现，同伴互动对难度大的任务（如思辨任务）有更显著的促进作用，不仅能带来意义协商和形式协商，还能够让学生有机会锻炼思辨技能。同伴互动使学习者更容易发现自己听力过程中的问题，促使他们施加注意，从而有利于听力能力的发展（王艳 2019）。

以上教学法是按照时间顺序回顾的，那么是不是新出现的教学法就一定好于之前的教学法？我认为，无论什么教学法都有优点和缺点，我们应该根据教学目标、教学内容和学生情况，选择合适的方法。练精听，用文本段落录音去听写，没问题；当然，用原声音视频也可以。原声材料还可以用作泛听，让学生练习听大意，学会容忍自己有听不懂的情况出现，并知道用后面的信息弥补；课堂可以播放听力材料、对答案，但是不能一味这样测试，令学生既不知道困难产生的原因，也不知道怎样去解决。此外，还应知道策略法是教会学生怎样去听，但是策略本身并不能取代听力练习。没有大量的练习，策略就是空中楼阁。教师应充分了解各种方法，扬长避短，灵活运用。

本书各章节均根据具体目标设计了活动实例，这些实例来自笔者的教学实践，仅作为示例，远不是最好的，相信广大教师读者都有无穷的智慧，会根据自己的课堂设计出更精彩的活动方案。

1.3.5 激发学习兴趣

在二语习得中，情感因素是指那些与学习者个人相关的情绪、感觉或者态度等制约行为的因素。关注情感因素能使学习更加有效，一方面可以创造和利用正向的、有促进作用的情感（如自尊、移情、动机，等等）促进语言学习，另一方面要克服负面情感（焦虑、恐惧、压力、压抑，等等）的不利影响(Oatley & Jenkins 1996：2)。在活动设计中，可以从以下几个方面考虑，来激发学生的学习兴趣。

第一，营造语言学习的真实场景。研究表明，集中精力听外语，在几分钟后就会产生疲劳。传统教学中类似测试的教学模式形式单一，时间一长，学生极易产生倦怠，注意力降低，学习兴趣下降甚至丧失。如果在课堂上模拟真实的交际场景，设计真实的交际任务，创造与之契合的交际氛围，不但有趣，而且也能让学生体验到听力的实际运用。第二，选择新颖的话题和材料。选材和任务设置应与当今时代热点和学生需求紧密联系。实践证明，这样的选材和活动更受学生欢迎。第三，适当设置有挑战性的活动。不论学生的水平处于哪个阶段，教师都可以用难度稍高一些的任务和活动来激发学生的好胜心和求知欲。第四，注意活动类型的创新和变化。青年学生喜欢新鲜事物，具有好奇心，不喜欢一成不变，课堂的变化能吸引他们的注意。第五，注意个体差异。比如，教师对焦虑感强的学生要善于引导并设法增强其自信。遇到难点，教师可让学生们先相互讨论再个人发言；或者教师说一半，让学生接一半；或者让一个学生开个头，余下部分由其他学生共同完成，等等。此外，经常找机会表扬和鼓励暂时落后的学习者，让他们也有成就感。这种内在的"成就动机"对人的激励往往有意想不到的巨大作用。本书的活动设计力求体现上述的一个或几个方面。

1.4　怎样使用这本书？

本书的第一章为绪论，第二到第六章分别为理解型听力活动、思辨听力活动、跨文化听力活动、学术听力活动和欣赏型听力活动。这样安排章节既是从英语专业《国标》和大学外语《指南》中要求的能力出发，也是借鉴了 Rost（2002）和 Lucas（2008）对听力目的的分类。每章由四个部分组成。第一部分为情境案例，从教师的视角讲述与这一章主题相关的真实故事，旨在触发读者相似的经验，引起思考。第二部分呈现的是与本章主题相关的理论框架，为后面制定教学目标打下基础。第三部分是为实现本章所讨论的能力而设定的具体教学目标，是基于听力研究领域的成果和笔者的听力教学实践所做出的设计。第四部分为教学设计实例，包括要点讲解、课前准备、活动实例、音视频文本、变化与拓展等五个小部分。

教师可以根据自己院校的情况，选择其中的章节和自己使用的教材配合使用，达成教学目标。本书活动设计中的听力材料，有的改编自《大学思辨英语教程视听说》教材，有的改编自开放的网络资源。活动实例是作为例子，用来说明实现目标的方法，教师完全可以根据自己的教学目标和学情，做出自己的创造。

第二章　理解型听力活动

2.1　理解型听力的情境案例

　　张老师教英语已经差不多 10 年了，教英语听力课也有 5 年了，已经具备了比较丰富的教学经验。她热爱听力教学，不但对每堂教学都能做到认真准备，而且常常在课上补充一些有趣的视听材料。但是，在一次会议交流中，她却向我说起这样的困惑：

　　"我发现有几个矛盾。一个是'想'与'做'的矛盾。有相当一部分学生，他们也很想提高自己的听力水平，而且还想很快见效。我在教学中发现，学生们最感兴趣的是听力学习的方法和策略。有一天，有位学生甚至问我会不会教'不用听懂，就能选对'的策略，我听了非常诧异。我认为听力是需要多听多练才能掌握的技能，方法和策略再好，也不能取代练习啊，而且策略也不是万能的。可是，怎样才能让学生认同我的观点呢？另一个矛盾就是应该以应试为目标还是以提高能力为目标。一些学生好像还是改不了在中学时养成的应试心理。如果我的教学和考试关系不大，他们就不感兴趣，我有时真觉得自己吃力不讨好。怎样才能让他们提高听力学习积极性？有的老师说教听力最轻松，可我怎么觉得不好教呢？"

　　张老师的困惑反映出了听力教学中的典型问题。学生为什么视方法与策略为捷径？怎样提高听力能力从而再也不惧怕考试？在这一章中，我们将聚焦如何提高二语听力理解能力，希望这一章的内容能帮助找到这些问题的解答。在介绍具体的听力课堂活动设计之前，我们先回顾听力理解的理论框架，然后确立教学目标。听力课堂活动针对教学目标而设计，包括要点讲解、课前准备、活动实例、音视频文本、变化与拓展等环节。

2.2 理解型听力的理论框架

2.2.1 理解型听力的定义

在二语听力中，理解是最基础也是最首要的目标。虽然人们常常把"听力"和"听力理解"两个词等同起来使用，但是"理解"这个词本身其实有其专指的含义。理解是指将语言与人脑中的概念以及现实世界中的参照物形成关联的过程（Sanders & Gernsbacher 2004）。理解的目标是将听到的概念在大脑中形成有逻辑、有条理的心理表征（Rost 2011）。听者处理所听到的语言信号，确认说话人想要表达的意思。听力理解，用简单的话来说，就是"听懂"口头语言。

从听的不同目的来看，理解型听力以获取知识、了解信息为目的，而不是判断和评价它们。理解也是传统听力教学的主要目标。思辨听力、跨文化听力和学术听力等活动，都要以理解为基础。没有理解作为基础，听力的高级活动很难顺利进行。

2.2.2 听力理解模型

要深入了解听力理解是什么，必须探究其过程。口头语言是怎样被听懂的？听是人类高度复杂的认知和行为过程。出于研究的目的，人们将这一复杂的过程分为多个阶段，也提出了多个模型。其中，影响力比较广的是以下这些模型。

"自下而上"的模型在 20 世纪 40—50 年代就已经发展起来。这一模型从信息传递的角度看待听力理解，认为听力理解就是听者先听到音素，再组合成词汇，再形成词组、句子，最后句子组合在一起形成意思和概念。按照这一模型，听的过程就是一个自下而上、从低往高流动的层级结构。信息的发出者（说话人）把要传递的信号进行编码，经过传递渠道，被信息的接收人（听者）解码（Shannon & Weaver 1949）。这种"自下而上"的方式又被称为数据驱动型的处理方式（Flowerdew & Miller 2005）。

在 20 世纪 80—90 年代，人们转而关注听者大脑中已有的知识对理解的作用，提出了"自上而下"的模型。根据这一模型，人们在听力理解过程中会使用存储在大脑中的"图式""框架"和"脚本"来帮助理解，而不是依赖对所听到的音或者词汇的处理。这一模型认为，理解是一个从高到低、从大到小的解构过程。听者凭借自己的情境信息、话题知识和体裁知识，去假设、预测和推断说话人的意思，弥补"自下而上"理解中在微观层面理解上的不足。也就是说，即便有些音没有听清、有个别词汇的意思不知道，听者也能够通过大脑中的先有知识，推断出说话人的意思。这种"自上而下"的方式又被称为概念驱动型的处理方式（Flowerdew & Miller 2005）。

很显然，这两种处理模式中的任何一种都不能全面反映听力理解的复杂过程。相反，成功有效的听力理解需要这两种过程的共同参与。这两种模型最初来源于对阅读的研究，后来 McClelland & Rumelhart（1981）在对阅读的研究中提出交互模型，认为"自下而上"的处理过程和"自上而下"的处理过程是相互作用、相互制约的。事实上，在听力理解中也是如此，两种处理模式是需要平衡和互补的。

Anderson（2000）的听力理解三阶段模型也具有较大的影响力。这一模型认为，二语听力理解包括感知处理、解析和使用等三个阶段。在感知处理阶段，听者将注意力集中于口头语言信号，并保留一部分在短时记忆中进行初级加工。短时记忆的容量有限，新信息不断被存入短时记忆，原有的信息不断被取代。这一阶段主要处理的是语音切分和音素辨别等问题。第二阶段是解析。词汇被识别出来，和长时记忆中的表征相匹配，形成意义的基本单元——命题。在这一阶段，听者会使用这门语言的语法知识和语义线索来进行解析。第三阶段是使用。命题与长时记忆中的其他信息和概念相结合，与原有的概念和图式形成关联。在听的过程中，这三个阶段相互关联，不断切换，形成循环。

2.2.3　影响二语听力理解的因素

在教学中我们不难发现，提高学习者的听力理解能力并非易事。那么，影响二语学习者听力理解的因素有哪些？过去 40 年来，许多学者（如 Boyle 1984；

Dunkel 1991；Rubin 1994；Vandergrift 2007）都对此做过研究。Boyle（1984）将影响二语听力理解的因素分为听者的因素、来自说话者的因素以及来自听力材料和媒介的因素。Dunkel（1991）将影响因素分为人脑之内的因素和人脑之外的因素，简称内部因素和外部因素。Rubin（1994）回顾了130篇听力实证研究，划分出五类因素，即文本特征、说话人特征、任务特征、听者特征和过程特征。Vandergrift（2007）则从另一个角度，把影响听力理解的因素分为认知因素和社会−心理因素。

综合这些研究结果，我们可以把影响因素分为学习者内部因素和学习者外部因素（Liu 2003）。学习者内部因素还可分为不可变因素和可变因素（王艳2014），参见表2.1。

表2.1 影响二语听力理解的因素

学习者内部因素		学习者外部因素
不可变因素	**可变因素**	
性别 年龄 母语 智力 学能等	**认知**：二语知识（如语音、词汇、语法、语篇知识等）、世界知识、记忆、注意力、策略（认知和元认知）等； **情感**：态度、动机、感情、信心、个性、努力、焦虑等； **社会**：语用知识、副语言知识、社会文化知识等。	**文本**：语速、停顿、犹豫、句法修饰、重音、节奏、冗余变化、文本类型等； **说话人**：是否专业、说话风格和特点、说话人性别等； **任务**：任务类型、听力目标等。

（王艳 2014：31）

可变因素包括认知因素、情感因素和社会因素三个层面。其中，认知因素包括二语知识（如语音、词汇、语法、语篇知识等）、世界知识、记忆、注意力、策略等；情感因素包括态度、动机、感情、信心、个性、努力、焦虑等；社会因素包括语用知识、副语言知识（如身势语）和社会文化知识等。不可变因素包括性别、年龄、母语、智力、学能等。这里，不可变因素是学习者已经具备的个人特征，而可变因素是教师和学习者通常更感兴趣的、通过教学能起到改善作用的那些因素（Wen & Johnson 1997）。

学习者外部因素与听力文本特征、说话人、听力任务等有关。文本特征包括语速、停顿、犹豫、句法修饰、重音、节奏、冗余变化和文本类型等；说话人的特征包括是否专业、说话风格和特点、说话人性别等；任务特征包括任务类型和听力目标等。

可变与不可变，本质上是相对的。有些因素可能通过长时间学习会发生改变，而在一段时间内基本上处于稳定的水平（如学能）。目前这样分类是为了充分认识影响因素的本质，更好地考虑教学的主体（即学习者），从而提出针对性和有效性更强的教学目标。

2.3 理解型听力的教学目标

基于对听力理解过程的分析和影响因素的分类，理解型听力教学的目标应着重夯实听力基本技能，加强听力策略训练，拓展知识和语音记忆能力，兼顾情感和社会因素。

2.3.1 加强语音能力

听力理解过程所处理的是语言的声音信号。虽然发音和听音是语音能力不可分割且相互影响的两个方面，但是在听力课堂上讲的语音能力，着重指语音的接收和感知。教学重点可包括音的听辨、韵律特征辨析、连续语流的切分，以及熟悉常见英语变体的口音。

音的听辨是指学习者应熟悉所学语言的语音系统，可以判别相似的音，对含有相似音的单词不会混淆，如 feet 和 fit；应知道哪些音母语中没有，如英文中的 /θ/，进而能与母语中相近的音加以区别，如能分辨出 /θɪŋk/ 和 /sɪŋk/ 是不同的词；应知道哪些组合英语中没有，如英语中有 /sl/ 的发音组合，但是没有 /pw/ 的发音组合。

韵律是语言交流中传达意图的重要工具，不可忽视。韵律特征是指语调、节奏这样的特征，它们会影响句子的意思。我们知道，说话人往往通过调整音高、响度、音质和说话速度等来实现意图的传达。Monrad-Krohn（1947）将韵律分为语言韵律和情感韵律。语言韵律是指语调、节奏、重读、停顿等，情感韵律则是指话语中情感的表达。举例来说，话语的开头和结尾常常语调不同；句子的重音处往往是强调；提出建议与传达命令有明显的升降调区别；而高兴、气愤、悲伤、恐惧等情绪从音高、语速等方面也能够感受到。可通过听原声材料，结合语境，将上述韵律特征逐一分析、听练，逐步培养语感。

连续语流的切分是一个难点。在使用母语交流时，我们能轻松识别说话人话语中的一个个词汇，这完全是因为我们熟悉这一语言。对于陌生的语言，我们听到的其实是连续不断的语音流，并不知道如何切分。确认语音流中词汇的边界，乃是理解词汇的基础，更是理解话语的基础（Anderson 2000）。听者在词汇识别中的两大任务，就是确认词汇边界并激活有关词汇意思的知识。其中，确认词汇边界非常关键（Rost 2002）。词汇识别常常是听力理解中最困难的一个过程（Cutler 1997）。正是因为这样，语音流的切分被看成是成功解码的最重要因素之一（Al-jasser 2008）。对初级和中级水平的学习者来说，掌握语音流的切分能力尤为重要。

随着英语作为通用语在全球多个领域被广泛使用，说英语的人来自更多不同的国家，而不仅限于以英语作为母语的国家。人们使用英语作为交流的媒介，他们的英语发音不可避免地会受到各自母语发音的影响。即便是以英语作为母语的人，也可能因地域、种族等原因带上口音。应让学习者有机会熟悉常见英语变体的发音系统，练习听懂带有口音的英语。综上所述，提高语音能力是听力理解教学的首要目标。

2.3.2　扩大听力词汇量

在众多影响听力理解的因素中，听力词汇量的影响最大，也最直接（王艳 2014）。二语听力学习者所反映的听力理解困难，也以生词为多。大力提升听力词汇量，是提高听力理解能力的最有效途径。那么，到底需要多大词汇量才能达到理解？

我们所听的材料含有多少已知词汇，可用词汇覆盖率（Lexical Coverage）来衡量，即已知的词汇占文本总词汇量的百分比。在阅读理解中，达到基本理解的词汇覆盖率为 95%；要达到充分理解，词汇覆盖率应达到 98%（Hu & Nation 2000）。也就是说，在每 100 个词中，只有两个是生词。Laufer & Ravenhorst-Kalovski（2010）也将 95% 和 98% 分别设为最低理解和最佳理解的两个门槛值。有人认为，在听力理解中，学习者在听词汇覆盖率为 80%—89% 的材料时，如果加上一些策略使用，也能达到足够的理解（Bonk 2000）。但 Schmitt（2008）的研究反对这一结论，他证明学习者拥有 95% 的词汇覆盖率才能达到足够理解。Van Zeeland & Schmitt（2013）认为，听力理解所需要的词汇覆盖率与听者所需要的理解程度有关。98% 的词汇覆盖率可以帮助听者达到很高的理解程度，而 95% 的词汇覆盖率是听者能够实现"很好但是并不必须完全理解"的一个值。那么，这两个值分别对应多大词汇量呢？换句话说，如果我们要让学生达到足够理解或完全理解，分别需要掌握多少词汇？

经过基于语料库的研究，对于口头语言要达到 95% 的词汇覆盖率，相当于要掌握 3000 个词族加上专有名词和边缘词汇；要达到 98% 的词汇覆盖率，相当于要掌握 6000—7000 个词族加上专有名词和边缘词汇（Nation 2006；Webb & Rodgers 2009a，2009b）。词族是指一组词，包含核心词和经过屈折或派生变化的词。例如，move、moving、movable、movement 都算作一个词族，因为只要知道 move 的意思，其他几个词都比较容易辨认和理解。我国高考英语要求的词汇量是 3500，公共外语英语四级要求 4200，六级要求 5500，专四的要求是 6000，专八的要求是不低于 8000。但是这个数量是单词数，不是词族。所以，按照上面 95% 的词汇覆盖率的要求，我国学习者的词汇缺口还很大（词族和词汇量的换算值，因是高频词还是低频词而有不同，可参看本书学术型听力这一章。）

需要注意的是，一般的词汇量都是基于阅读来测试的，并不是学习者能听懂的词汇量。如果把词汇量分为阅读词汇量（看得懂的词汇的数量）和听力词汇量（听得懂的词汇的数量），那么我们应该知道，这两者并不等同。据刘思（1995）对中国外语学习者的研究，他们的听力词汇量只有阅读词汇量的一半多一点。随着近年来学习者听说水平的提高，这个比例应有提高。但不可否认的是，学习者常常发现这样一个现象：听不懂某一个词，而之后看到这个词却发现原来认识。提高听力词汇量，是学习者极为关心，也是听力教学应重点解决的问题。

2.3.3　有效使用策略

听不是被动地接收声音信号，而是主动地调用一切资源去获取说话人所传递的信息。策略能力，对学习者来说并不陌生。策略是指学习者在学习和使用语言时有意识地采取方法以达成目标。这个词在中文里的核心意思是根据具体情况制定方式方法。在英文中，strategy 指为达成目标而计划的一系列行动以及这种计划能力。最初，Canale & Swain（1980）提出的策略能力（strategic competence）是交际能力（communicative competence）的组成部分，是指在交际过程中识别并修补交际失败的一种能力。外语学习者因为语言能力不够，难免在交流中遇到问题，他们就需要这样一种能力来保证交流的顺利进行。后来，O'Malley & Chamot（1990）提出的学习策略是指二语学习者专门用来帮助理解、学习和保存信息的想法与行为。同样地，掌握听力策略，既指听者能使用一些方法来更加有效地理解所听信息，也指听者具备在交流中解决听力困难的能力。

在过去的 20 年中，在有关听力策略的研究领域有了一系列发现。例如：善听者比不善听者更会使用策略；听力策略是可教的；如果不教，听力策略并非人人都能掌握，在课堂上讲授听力策略行之有效；如果将各种策略结合起来使用，听力理解的表现会更好，等等（Graham & Macaro 2008；Siegel 2014；Vandergrift & Tafaghodtari 2010）。虽然策略能力是一种非语言能力，但是具备这种能力能够让学习者学会管理听的过程，应对听力困难。事实上，随着听力教学理念的改变，教师已经普遍认可策略原本就应该是听力教学的重要目标之一。

听力策略可分为元认知策略、认知策略和社会-情感策略（O'Malley & Chamot 1990）。元认知策略是指学习者管理和监督自己策略的使用，包括计划、监控和评价自己的听力过程，并能够应对这一过程中出现的问题。认知策略是指直接用来处理所听信息、目的在于改善理解的大脑认知活动，包括推断、预测、总结、翻译、重复、联想，等等。社会-情感策略指寻求他人帮助、与他人互动等社会策略，以及降低焦虑、自我鼓励等自身情感控制策略。课堂上可以通过增强策略意识、展示策略使用、提供策略练习、评估策略效果等一系列方法（Rubin et al. 2007）来实现提高策略能力的教学目标。有关策略能力的活动设计在《英语听力教学与研究》（王艳 2012）的第五章有详细论述和案例，本书不再赘述。

2.3.4　善用知识储备

几乎所有知识的学习，都建立在从前的经验和知识的基础上。如果没有知识和经验的基础去理解外语，是不可想象的。人们在使用外语进行交流的时候，需要运用已经存在于大脑中的各种知识，除了有关外语的知识，还有常识和经验。学界对这些知识有不同的提法，如背景知识、话题知识、世界知识或先有知识。尽管提法不同，但是本质上都是指学习者大脑中已有的、有关这个世界、这个话题或者相关背景的知识。这些知识在听力理解中发挥着不可或缺的作用。

从"理解"的定义可以知道，理解的关键在于听懂说话人想要表达的意思。听者将听到的概念在大脑中形成合乎逻辑的、连贯的心理表征。这一建构的过程要求听者接收的新信息与大脑中已有的旧信息形成关联（Rost 2011）。如果能够顺利激活大脑中相关的知识和经验，就有利于听者去理解说话人所指的现实世界中的参照物，而不是停留在语言和概念层面。

研究发现，成功的听者善于使用他们已有的知识来理解话语，而不成功的听者则容易忽略对此知识的使用（Bacon 1992）。Chiang & Dunkel（1992）和 Schmidt-Rinehart（1994）都发现，学习者听话题熟悉的讲座，理解得更好。他们认为，是听者已有知识的存在使他们的理解更为顺畅。已有知识是促进听力理解的一个强大因素。Buck（2001）认为，听是听者积极构建意义的过程，这个过程取决于听者如何利用所知道的一切知识和经验。

教学上一般采用听前练习来激活话题或背景知识。实际上，每个听者有关话题的背景知识是不一样的。教师可以在各个层面上开展主动构建意义的活动，可结合元认知策略和认知策略的教学。合作和互动也是可以尝试的新方式。

2.3.5　拓展语音记忆

语音记忆或短时语音记忆（Phonological Short-term Memory），对听力理解有重要的影响(Jacquemot & Scott 2006)。语音记忆是工作记忆的一部分。早年，记忆被分为长时记忆和短时记忆，主要用来区别是临时存储还是长期存储。近年来，心理学领域更倾向于把短时记忆称为工作记忆，以体现它并不只是短暂地、被动地存储信息，而是也能在复杂的认知活动中起到主动地存储和管理信息的功能。有相关研究提出，工作记忆模型含有中央处理器、语音回路、视觉–空间模板和情节缓冲（Gathercole & Baddeley 1993；Baddeley & Hitch 1974）。其中，语音回路专门负责声音信息的存储和刷新。

语音记忆是指识别和记忆语音单元及其出现顺序的能力（O'Brien et al. 2007）。语音记忆所提供的存储帮助保持信息，以供大脑的进一步加工。它能够通过暂时保持语音痕迹，直至更长久的表征形成。语音记忆在儿童学习新词的时候发挥着强大的作用，它甚至被 Baddeley 等(1974) 称为"语言学习机制"。在听力理解中，听者必须把听到的声音信号保持在记忆中，且要保持足够长的时间让其来得及完成对语言流的感知和切分、对词汇的识别、对句子或语篇意思的构建。可见，语音记忆在二语听力理解过程中发挥着至关重要的作用。拓展语音记忆，有助于从根本上改善理解的过程。

2.3.6　学会合作互动

合作听力，顾名思义，就是结成对子或者以小组形式，与他人一起练习听力。与一个人独自去听相比，合作听力多了口头互动、信息共享和相互支持。正如前文指出的，每个人的知识储备都不一样。听前的对子和小组讨论，能够在更广的范围内激活背景知识，有助于听前的计划。听后的讨论互动则有更多的好处。学生可以就自己听不懂的地方提出疑问，比较对方的回答和自己的理解，还可以复述所听的内容来说明理由。这种相互间的询问、核对、澄清和解释，能够帮助听者发现自己的问题，弥补自己理解的不足，纠正可能错误的假设，从而确定在下一遍听的时候应该选择在哪里重点施加注意。

合作听力促使学习者对自己的理解过程加以审视。无论合作伙伴给出的想法是否正确，合作双方都获得了独自聆听时所没有的东西，这就是反馈。我们知道，外语听力课堂基本都采用单向聆听方式，而在单向听力中，听者是无法获得说话人反馈的。理解得怎么样，哪里听错了，一般是靠核对练习答案来检查。很多时候，核对答案发现自己错了，却并不知道错在哪里。合作听力能让学习者发现问题所在，从而找到自己的不足。

合作听力还可以起到调节情绪、降低焦虑的作用。听前的讨论能活跃气氛，提高学习动机和参与度，避免独自聆听时的倦怠；听后回答问题出错也不用过于担心个人丢面子，因为答案是对子和小组在完成任务时共同做出的。

然而，多年来我国对学生合作能力的培养仍旧不足。学外语的学生不是不可以独自埋头苦读，而是不应忽视互动合作在语言学习和语言交流中的作用。听力课堂可通过开展合作型听力活动，在促进学生听力理解能力的同时，提高其与人合作的意识和能力。

2.4　理解型听力教学设计实例

这一部分是针对教学目标而做的教学设计实例。在每个设计中，先讲解设计所依据的知识要点，再介绍可准备的材料和活动形式，然后给出教学活动实例，实例中使用的音视频文本和材料来源也一并附上，最后是活动的变化与拓展，主要是给教师在不同情境下使用该活动设计提供思路以及一些注意事项。

2.4.1　理解型听力活动设计一：准确感知和切分语音流

1）要点讲解

在连续的语流中确认或定位词汇边界的能力被称作词汇切分能力（Lexical Segmentation Ability）（Field 2003；Al-jasser 2008）。另有一些学者（如 Muter & Diethelm 2001）也把它叫做语音切分能力（Phonological Segmentation Ability）。本质上，它是指切分语音流的能力。Dejean de la Batie & Bradley（1995）曾指出，

在确定词汇边界的时候，词汇知识和语音知识都有制约作用。因此，两种名称都有合理之处。也可以说，这一过程始于对语音的处理，止于对词汇的识别。词汇切分是一种解码的过程。听者在此过程中分析语音流中的声音，并把它们与记忆中的词汇或句法知识相匹配，最终得到话语的字面意思。实际上，词汇切分能力这一概念反映了学习者在语言理解中使用语音知识、词汇知识和句法知识的综合能力。

既然语流是连续的，那么根据什么线索来切分就成为关键。一个词和其他词一起出现在句子中，其相邻处的发音，可能不变，也可能发生变化，会出现音的增减，甚至音的消失。当语速快的时候，这种现象尤其普遍。词的发音通常受到相邻词汇发音的制约。因为语速快，人们并不愿意频繁更换口腔里的发音位置，而是更愿意用原来的位置或者折中的位置，把一些音连起来发，这样既节省时间，又节省力气。另一个原因是英语是一种以重音计时的语言（a stress-timed language）。为保持节奏，说话人通过压缩重音单元之间的音节，以协助发音。

从发音上分析，在词汇的边界常有三类音变情况。第一类是音素的发音没有变化，但是生成了新的音节，如连读。上一个词结尾的辅音和下一个词开头的元音连在一起发音，如在 a lot of 中的 lot 和 of 之间。第二类是音的删减。当两个词的相邻处是两个辅音，其中一个辅音的发音会减弱或消失，如 "Did he do his homework?" 这句中的 he，/h/ 的发音很弱，有时消失；在 best gift 和 old time 这两例中也是如此，划线处的发音几乎听不到。相邻的若为元音，也有类似情况，如 see it 中两个词的连接处。第三类是有新的音产生。例如，两个元音中有滑动，如在 "I am what I am." 中，I 和 am 的连接处有 /j/ 音的出现，而在 the idea of 中，idea 和 of 中间有一个 /r/ 音。

2）课前准备

用于练习感知和切分语音流的材料并不难找，只要是清晰而自然的语流，都可以用来做例子。需要注意包含如上文所述的典型类别，并选取不同语速的材料。一般来说，语速越快，感知和切分的难度越大。可以参考下例选择合适的材料并设计好练习。

(1) 准备语音流切分中的典型音变例子，例如：

- *uhz* good *uhz* it gets (as good as it gets)
- mac *n* cheese (mac and cheese)
- *uh cuppa* coffee (a cup of coffee)
- I *hafta* go. (I have to go.)
- Children *a* play (children at play)
- *Tabi r na tabi* (to be or not to be)
- *un* apple a day (an apple a day)
- *Gimme* your hand. (Give me your hand.)
- *Booka da* month (book of the month)
- hole *n* one (hole in one)
- *Whaddya* want? (What do you want?)
- *Whatja* say? (What did you say?)

(选自 Brown 2012)

(2) 将语音流切分中的典型音变类型制作成练习。例如，要求学生判断词汇边界是否增加了 /j/ 或 /w/，在相应的空格内打钩。

Word/Phrase	/j/	/w/
allow us		✓
by association	✓	
Hello Ann		✓
high over	✓	
way out	✓	
you ask		✓

(3) 准备一段电影或电视剧里的英文对话片段（选 8—10 句），选择话题难度适中、句子长度适中、话轮较多的片段。不要含有太多的生僻词汇。将对话句子挖空制作成听写填空题。

3）活动实例

切分语音流的常用活动是听写。可由教师说出词的组合，让学生听写，也可以听原声材料的片段，听写其中的句子。这里介绍一个可把听音和发音结合起来，也能增加课堂乐趣的活动：传话游戏。

听前

让全班学生按座位就近分成几列，每列尽量相同的人数，如四列五排。自然班的人数不一定正好齐整，所以有一列两列是四排的也没有问题。目的是做到每列传话的次数尽量均等。安排好后，教师举例展示活动方法。

听中

本例中，教师用 20 个词组来做传话游戏（词组见下表）。教师小声说出词组，第一排的同学听到后转身说给第二排的人，第二排听到后转身说给第三排的同学，以此类推，最后一位同学写下这个词。每轮练习 5 个，总共 4 轮。每完成一轮，请每组最后一位同学上来，将听到的词组写在黑板上。全部完成后，教师将所有词组的正确形式显示于幻灯，让学生核对。接下来，教师将每个词组的音标依次显示在屏幕上，讲解边界处的发音变化，让学生体会所听到的音变并将听错或说错的词组多练习几遍。

听后

经过练习，学生对词汇相邻处的音变规律已有所领会，这时教师可较为系统地介绍语音流切分的相关知识，补充其他练习，如课前准备材料中的（1）或（2）。课后作业可以布置为影视片段配音。

4）音视频文本

	Phrase	Connected Speech
1	top person	/tɒpːɜːsən/
2	Bob Brown	/bɒbːraʊn/
3	hot time	/hɒtːaɪm/
4	dead drunk	/dedːrʌŋk/
5	big guy	/bɪɡːaɪ/

（待续）

（续表）

	Phrase	Connected Speech
6	off flavor	/ɒfːleɪvə/
7	of victory	/əvːɪktri/
8	less stress	/lesːtres/
9	these zebras	/ðiːzːiːbrəz/
10	Irish sheep	/aɪrɪʃːiːp/
11	reach Charleston	/riːtʃːɑːlstən/
12	change jeans	/tʃeɪndʒːiːnz/
13	a good dog	/əgʊdːɒg/
14	a small lion	/əsmɔːlːaɪjən/
15	a big gorilla	/əbɪgːərɪlə/
16	a cute tiger	/əkjuːtːaɪgə/
17	a strange giraffe	/əstreɪndʒːərɑːf/
18	a handsome monkey	/əhænsəmːʌŋki/
19	a black cat	/əblækːæt/
20	a nice snail	/ənaɪsːneɪl/

（改编自 Brown 2012）

5）变化与拓展

在课堂时间比较紧的情况下，可用准备材料（3），直接用原声音视频来做练习。先听一遍（如果视频片段有字幕则需关闭），然后发放听写练习。将音视频播放第二遍，在每句之后暂停，让学生完成听写。最后再连续播放一遍供检查。请学生们相互批改，如有不同，需回忆并说出自己听到了什么。接下来，教师将听写的正确文本显示出来，请学生们模仿发音，说出词汇边界处的音变情况，最后教师系统讲解感知和切分语音流的知识。

为电影或电视剧片段配音是一项受学生欢迎的活动。原声的语速通常比学生的语速快，因此，当经过多次聆听、模仿语音语调、对口型等练习，最终能成功为某个片段配音之后，学生对语音流的感知和切分能力也会大有提高。

在平时说英语的时候，如果注意自然语流中词汇边界的音变特征，也会促使我们熟悉这一规律，从而在听的时候能更准确地感知。所以，听音和发音的活动常常不分彼此。教师也应时常注意学生的口语，提醒并纠正学生在词汇边界的不正确发音。

2.4.2　理解型听力活动设计二：熟悉常见的英语口音

1）要点讲解

在全球化日益发展的今天，英语已成为一种国际通用语言。在对外交流中，我们常常遇到交际对方所说的英语带有口音的情况。据 2021 年的最新统计，全球使用英语作为官方语言和第二语言的人数为 13.5 亿人，这个数字还并不包含那些不以英语为官方语言和第二语言但能够使用英语进行交流的人。若把这个群体也计算进去，全球使用英语者已超过 20 亿人，远超以英语为母语国家的人口总数。英语已经成为母语不同的人用来相互交流的语言。

以英语为母语或官方语言的国家有不同的英语变体，在发音上有比较明显的口音特征，如英式英语、美式英语、澳大利亚英语、新加坡英语、印度英语、南非英语，等等。即便是英语本族语者，也因生活地域不同而具有口音的区别，如我们熟悉的标准美式发音叫 General American（GenAm），但是美国人说的英语也有西北部、南部和东部口音等的分别。英式英语的标准口音曾被称作 RP（Received Pronunciation），其他口音包括 Cockney（伦敦土音）、Estuary（英国东南部口音）、Brummie（伯明翰口音）等，以及威尔士英语和苏格兰英语等不同口音。

当其他国家和地区的英语非本族语者说英语时，也会因为母语的影响而带上口音。当听到带有口音的英语时，除了理解上的困难，还不可避免地遭遇跨文化问题。学习者不但应经常聆听有口音的听力材料，熟悉常见的口音，还应该对带有不同口音的说话者抱有平等和尊重的态度。

2）课前准备

（1）准备英语在全球语言使用中的大致分布资料，以及英语作为通用语的发展简况。书面材料或音视频材料均可。

（2）准备不同英语变体的音视频材料，除了英式英语、美式英语，澳大利亚英语、新西兰英语的听力材料外，还可准备其他英语变体如新加坡英语、印度英语等的音视频，并总结发音规律。

（3）准备非本族语者说英语的音视频片段，包括日本人说英语、法国人说英语等，并总结发音规律。

3）活动实例

听前

听前活动是听一个对话：在校园中，来自不同国家的几名大学新生聚在一起，聊着开学第一周的新感受。任务为听对话，辨别口音，判断说话人是否来自相同的国家和地区，体会不同英语变体的发音。

听中

主材料是一段新西兰口音的听力材料，语速不快，但是不熟悉新西兰口音的人通常会感觉口音比较陌生，甚至听不懂本来就熟知的词汇。先听一遍，再完成如下填空练习。

Workers who care for elderly people in _____ are poorly paid. A report by the Human Rights Commission to the Prime Minister recommended _____. Many are paid less than carers in public hospitals. It is not easy work. Many patients need help to wash, dress, walk and feed themselves. Some patients with _____ can be angry and difficult. Carers are mostly female and perhaps this is the reason for low pay. Health care workers who visit elderly people in their own homes are also poorly paid. They also do not get paid enough for _____ and travel.

再听一遍，听完后先请学生们与同桌核对答案并找出发音规律，再全班讨论。

听后

讲解新西兰英语发音规律，如 /e/ 常常发成 /i/，pen 听起来就像是 pin。可拓展到英式、美式、澳大利亚英语等英语变体的典型发音特征。

4）音视频文本

(1) First Week at University

What was your first week at university like? Here's what people in London said.

A: First week at university was really exciting and there's so much to look forward to and so…there's a new life ahead of you and you're looking at future plans and what am I going to be doing five years from now. But generally speaking, one word to sum it up, it is really, really excited about university life.

B: It was so exciting to have new experiences with new friends, feeling independent and free.

C: Basically I made lots of friends, which helped me live sociably in London and at this university. For me, it was a really great experience.

D: It was exciting and I was a little bit scared as well because it was completely different for me. And I tried to get new friends and new people and I managed within a short time to get acquainted with a number of people.

(2) Workers Caring for Elderly People

Workers who care for elderly people in rest homes are poorly paid. A report by the Human Rights Commission to the Prime Minister recommended better pay. Many are paid the minimum wage of $13.50 an hour while carers in public hospital get $3 to $5 an hour more. It is not easy work. Many patients need help to wash, dress, walk and feed themselves. Some patients with memory loss can be angry and difficult. Carers are mostly female and perhaps this is the reason for low pay.

Health care workers who visit elderly people in their own homes are also poorly paid. They also do not get paid enough for petrol and travel time. Some of these carers start work at 7 a.m., visiting people who need help to have a shower and get dressed. Then the health care worker visits again in the evening to help the patient get undressed for bed.

Other recommendations in the report include the need for more male workers. The report also recommended that countries like the Philippines where many carers come from, have good information about our qualifications. There are qualifications for health care workers and the report recommended that all workers have Level 3 qualifications within 18 months of starting a job.

The Prime Minister will now have to consider the report.

（说明：两篇听力音频可参考《大学思辨英语视听说》第 1 册第 1 单元和第 2 单元）

5）变化与拓展

听后活动中还可拓展有关全球语言分布的知识。可布置作业，让学生搜集各国语言使用的音视频资料，对使用英语作为母语、官方语言或第二语言的区域加强了解。还可以布置课后作业，让不同小组各自负责总结一种常见英语变体的发音规律，下一节课在课堂上分享。这样的活动能够很快帮助学生消除对不同变体口音的陌生感，提高识别能力。

2.4.3 理解型听力活动设计三：听力词汇学习

1）要点讲解

听力词汇的习得，与学习者施加的注意、词汇出现的频率和词汇的呈现方式等多种因素有关。学习者在课堂上有目的地学习词汇，与课后听英文歌曲、看英文电影时的附带习得，所投入的注意力并不一样。专门学习词汇，可以明晰化地兼顾词汇的音、形、义等各个方面，还可结合语境，把词汇的使用也包括进来。这样的学习显然更有效率。

那么，怎样才能更好地记忆词汇？重复有利于记忆。因此，教师应在活动设计中有意识地增加生词的重复频率，保证生词语音形式的多次输入。深度加工也有利于记忆。心理学研究认为，记忆是否牢固与大脑加工的程度有关。使用词汇就是一种加工。要习得一个生词，就要多使用它。相比直接用中文给出意思，不如通过给出英文解释、给近义词、做练习等来创造深度加工的机会。这样看来，传统听力课上一般只在听前过一遍生词的做法并不够。应围绕生词设计专门的任务，将词汇音、形、义的学习和使用融合起来，让学习者做深度加工。研究还表明，从生词学习的效率上看，只采用听入的模式，不如把读入和听入模式相结合好（Brown et al. 2008）。这也启发我们在活动设计中应尽可能采用多种模式呈现词汇。总之，建议在教学中加强听前和听后活动中的词汇学习，让听力词汇量有明显的增长。在此过程中，自始至终需要重视学生对词汇语音的记忆，以及语音与词义的匹配，这样才有可能使听力理解过程中的词汇识别和词义提取逐渐接近自动化。

2）课前准备

（1）将所学课文中的生词，用英文给出释义。

（2）为每个单词给出 1 个符合文中释义和用法的例句。该例句中最好不要含有其他生僻词。

（3）制作多种形式的练习。例如，先听句子释义，学习词汇，然后完成选词填空；或者先听词汇的释义，然后做选择题（可添加干扰项自制选择题）；或者让学生听该生词的使用例句，猜测词义，然后给出一些释义让学生从中选择准确的一项；或者先听该词的释义，然后完成词汇划线匹配题，等等。生词的读音、意思、在语境中的用法、拼写等都应给出。

3）活动实例

听前

词汇学习一般属于听前活动。教师解释所听材料中的生词（或者播放录音，有些教材已提供词汇释义的录音），然后将释义显示在幻灯上。请看下面的例子，生词部分已用黑体标出。讲解中尽量多次重复生词的发音。

1) **Momentum** is the force that is gained by movement.

2) To **plummet** means to fall suddenly and quickly from a high level or position.

3) If one amount or value is the **equivalent** of another, they are the same.

4) A **maverick** person is unusual, has different ideas and ways of behaving from other people, and is often very successful. **Maverick** can also be a noun.

5) A **visionary** person has clear ideas of what the world should be like in the future.

6) To **launch** means to start something, usually something big or important.

学完生词的音、形、义之后，完成下面的单词匹配练习，即选择左栏的词，填入右栏的句子。

	1. He is a weird, _____ detective.
equivalent	2. The wheel was allowed to roll down the slope, gathering
maverick	_____ as it went.
visionary	3. We will _____ a big advertising campaign to
launch	promote our new products.
plummet	4. The profit _____ from $49 million to $11 million.
momentum	5. Eight kilometers is roughly _____ to five miles.
	6. Under his _____ leadership, the city prospered.

听中

一般的理解型听力活动主要包含听主旨、听细节等任务。如果教师想突出生词的学习，就可以添加需要使用生词才能完成的内容。例如，此例中可要求用 100—150 个词来复述所听内容且必须含有所学的 6 个生词。

听后

我们常在听后活动中巩固语言点。可几周一次在听后活动中安排词汇活动，把几周中学到的词汇用填字游戏、拼词竞赛等方式进行复习。

4）音视频文本

Clear the rig, clear the rig!

Finally, it came up with such **momentum** that it just shot up clear through the top of the derrick.

The guides of crude oil shoot almost 200 feet into the air.

The Hamills were hoping for 50 barrels a day.

The well would soon be pumping out over 80,000, making the US the largest oil producer in the world. Oil production in the US instantly increases by 50%. Within a year, 500 oil companies are born, including Texaco and Gulf.

The price of oil **plummet**s from $2 a barrel to ₵3. It's cheaper than water. Cheap enough to turn into gasoline.

Around the turn of the century, millions of Americans live their entire lives within 50 miles of their home. Gasoline makes the US mobile in ways never thought possible. Today the average American drives the **equivalent** of two and a half round-trips to the moon.

One man will seize the opportunity in cheap oil and change the face of the nation.

Detroit, 1908, Henry Ford: **maverick**, **visionary**, obsessive…a man with a bad reputation. Recently let go by the company that will soon become Cadillac, he **launche**s his third attempt to build cars.

But these will be different.

There are only 8,000 cars in the US. Expensive toys for the wealthy, like owning a private jet today.

"There were dozens and dozens of small companies building cars that were essentially play things for the rich. They were notoriously unreliable; they were not standardized; they were hand-built, essentially. And if you were to own a car, you practically had to have your own mechanic on staff as well to keep the thing running."

Nobody's figured out how to make a car that's affordable and low-cost.

Henry Ford is about to change that. It won't just change how cars are made. It will change how everything is made.

5）变化与拓展

还有一种词汇练习的形式非常简洁好用，即给出单词释义中的生词，但是把用于解释该生词的核心词汇留空，做听力填空。教师朗读句子，学生做听写填空。举例如下（句末括号中的词为应填入的词）：

(1) Momentum is the _____ that is gained by movement. (force)

(2) To plummet means to _____ suddenly and quickly from a high level or position. (fall)

(3) If one amount or value is the equivalent of another, they are _____. (the same)

(4) A maverick person is _____, has different ideas and ways of behaving from other people, and is often very successful. Maverick can also be a noun. (unusual)

(5) A visionary person has _____ ideas of what the world should be like _____. (clear, in the future)

(6) To launch means to _____ something, usually something big or important. (start)

这个练习的特点是，所要听写的部分并不难，但是却能直接点明生词词义，易于记忆，同时生词的音和形也都学习到了。

在设计词汇练习时需要注意，一个词的释义往往不止一个，应给出适合听力材料语境的释义。另外，为生词设置的任务可以用幻灯放映，或者印成书面练习，但是尽量不要一上来就用视觉记忆的方式去接触词汇。在学习生词的活动中，最好第一遍单纯去听，加深语音记忆。也不必边听单词释义边做题，以免分散注意力。

2.4.4 理解型听力活动设计四：激活背景知识

1）要点讲解

听并不是单纯地解码语言信号。对大脑中知识的激活在很大程度上有助于语言编码的理解。那么，这些知识在大脑中是如何存放又是怎么提取的呢？图式理论（Schema Theory）认为，这些知识都是按照单元存放的。图式就是用来指这样的知识：物体以及物体之间的关系、情境、时间、事件的顺序、行动以及行动的顺序，等等。人从出生开始就经历各种事情，同时也在发展自己的知识图式，最终形成对现实的一套理论。这套理论不仅影响人们如何解释信息，还会随着新信息的接受而发生改变。图式代表我们各个层面的知识，从意识形态到文化现实，从看到某个字母后的神经反应到词的含义。各个层面的经验都有图式。图式就是我们的知识，所有我们的类别知识都植入在图式之中（Rumelhart 1980：41）。

除了物质世界的知识，社会文化知识也不例外。人们是通过激活相关的图式来处理新信息的。利用图式，人们可以预测、推理、判断和决策。根据"自上而下"的处理模式，听者运用大脑中已有的图式来预测文本的结构和内容。图式是长时记忆中的概念框架，用来组织和解释信息（Rumelhart 1980）。内容图式包括与话题有关的已有知识，形式图式包括与文本修辞有关的已有知识。听者普遍都有这样的经验，即熟悉的话题更容易懂。这就是内容图式在起作用。比如，听到"图书馆"，我们大脑里的相关图式被激活，我们就知道这是一幢建筑，里面有书籍、有看书的人，需要保持安静，等等。这些知识甚至成为假设和前提，听者和说话人都已达成共识。熟悉一个话题，往往意味着相关的背景知识更丰富，这些知识能弥补听者在预测所听内容、猜测生词等情况下的不足。

听母语的时候，我们往往是自动化地运用大脑中已经存在的知识，无需有意识地提醒。但是听外语的时候，激活已有的知识反而成为有目的、有意识的行为，比如在课堂上，我们通常用听前练习来帮助学生激活图式。听前练习经常采用的活动设计有热身讨论（抛出话题，问学生了解多少），情境引入（教师说一个小故事或新闻，引发学生对话题的思考），预习生词（提前学习所听材料中的生词），以及提前看任务（听前先把听力理解任务中的问答题或选择题的题干过一遍）等。此外，还可以让学生根据所听材料的体裁，对结构做一些预测。

2）课前准备

(1) 为所听材料准备好听前讨论题，用于激活与话题相关的知识。

(2) 准备图片或小视频，从视觉上激活话题，生动而且直观。

(3) 准备 A4 纸、记号笔等，用于小组活动时组间分享。

3）活动实例

听前

本例所用的教学材料是一篇有关数字影院的访谈。数字影院是一种新技术，人们希望通过它改变电影院的旧模样，使电影院不仅能放映电影，还能让更多的观众参与互动。这篇访谈语速较快，有不少专门词汇，难度偏大。听前，教师设计了两个开放式问题作为听前小组讨论题，旨在激活学生有关数字影院话题和访谈体裁的背景知识。题目如下：

• How much do you know about digital cinema?

• How much do you know about the structure of an interview?

教师把学生分成 5 人小组，要求讨论这两个题目并在纸上写出回答，时长限制为 15 分钟。15 分钟后，教师将全班（以 30 人为例）分为 6 组，编号为 1—6，依照 1-2-3-4-5-6-1 循环的次序，让每组将自己写着回答的纸交给下一组，同时收到上一组的回答。教师要求每小组评价其他组的回答，在特别好的回答上标上星号。一轮完成后所有回答交给老师讲评。

对于第一个问题，学生们大多是从拍摄技术的角度给出回答，教师随即引导学生又从影院的定位上进行思考。第二个问题引导学生回忆访谈的一般结构，通常包括开头的寒暄和介绍，然后是提问与回答，结尾处时常有总结。教师需要补充的是，抓住采访者提出的问题是听懂访谈节目的关键。教师还要提醒学生们注意积累听访谈类材料的知识和经验。

听中

本例是一个访谈类电视节目，话题有专业性，形式上一问一答，互动性强，可以设计理解大意和细节的活动，也可以设计通过语境理解俗语意思的听力策略练习，还可以用来设计思辨活动。无论何种练习，听前做一个充分的热身练习来激活背景知识，能够为之后的活动打下良好基础。

听后

听前活动中就让学生讨论了访谈类体裁的结构，因此在听后有必要呼应这方面的语言要点。本采访开头部分有寒暄和介绍：

- This is… and welcome to…
- I have with me…
- Thanks for having me.
- It's good to have you.

采访中的问题有：

- Four-walling has come a long way, hasn't it?
- What are some of the exact products, or services that you're offering inside the movie theater to give a movie-goer a different experience?
- What's your background?
- So, when does it become generally adopted across the board?
- How do you fit me in, how do you get me in?
- What does the future look like from here?

4）音视频文本

Digital Cinema Destination

Interviewer: Hi! This is Shelley Craft and welcome to SNN Live where the 14th Denial Be Rally in company invest-conference right here in Santa Monica, California. I have with me Bud Mayo, Digital Cinema Destinations

Corporation, symbol, DCIN. It is a publicly traded company. Bud, welcome to SNN live.

Interviewee: Thanks. Shelley. Thanks for having me.

Interviewer: It's good to have you. Okay, overview and then we'll go from there.

Interviewee: Basically, we're buying movie theaters from all around the country and transforming them into entertainment centers.

Interviewer: Four-walling has come a long way, hasn't it?

Interviewee: It sure has. En, what we're doing is making a difference by using all the digital tools that we've helped to create in previous businesses to change the choice for movie-goers, operas, pop-concerts, lecture series, documentaries. We're even curating many of those ourselves and participating in the downstreams, not just showing them in movie theaters and splitting the box with whoever owns it. So we're in a multi-level business, which is really giving a peek at the future exhibition as we see in this industry.

Interviewer: Okay. Let's take a step backwards to take three steps forward. Well, No 1. No 2: what are some of the exact products, or services that you're offering inside the movie theater to give a movie-goer a different experience?

Interviewee: Aside from making sure that every one of our theaters is completely digital, which means a crystal-clear image on the screen and better sound that doesn't deteriorate. We're now looking at choices of content they weren't available with film, which was a major problem, and so we're talking about playing product that fills seats that are empty during periods when those audiences aren't available to go. So why are we playing a child's movie at 10 o'clock at night or even at 7:30 at night when the kids are in school? Kids can't see them. Neither can their parents. So what do we do? We start thinking about what we're playing, when, just like cable stations do. Think about how they've programmed their day parts, and think about how they can be translated in the movie theaters in the digital world that we now live in, and that we as a management team helps to create.

Interviewer: What's your background?

Interviewee: IBM, Wall Street, just like you, and Down Street from Wall Street, literally and figuratively into the business, computer leasing, movie theaters on a goof and built a movie theater chain which is the largest independent metro New York clear-view cinemas, sold it to Cablevision, started the technology company to try to solve the problem that was essentially underutilized seat capacity and nobody's in a movie theater, Monday to Thursday, most of the year since the kids are home or at school. How do you fix that? Film had to get rid of, had to get out of the way, and make room for the digital era which every other form of media had already embraced.

Interviewer: So, when does it become generally adopted across the board? Let's quote straight.

Interviewee: 85% at the theaters that are really counted in the United States have already been converted. So the opportunity now is what you do with that technology. Now as the CEO of Cenodime, for years I was up on the podium, telling everybody in the industry: Guys, I know that I'm heading a technology company, but I'm telling you it's not about the technology. Think about what you're gonna do with that technology because that's what's gonna make a difference to you in your theaters.

Interviewer: Well, if I'm an advertiser, which I am, I would say how do you fit me in, how do you get me in, because that's what it's all about. You're trying to generate a new series of revenues that, okay you know, they have some advertising a little bit from left-over from the old days, but you're going to this screen with all of these people in there and you're going to be able to get a critical mess.

Interviewee: Well, not going to have a critical mess. I know exactly who they are, and what they like. Think about the Amazon model. That's what we're doing. People who enjoyed this also were interested in that and when we match content with audiences, we are on the right track. Along come sponsors and advertisers who are interested in interacting with those affinity groups. If I have a product, matching my product with the audiences that I'm interested in selling to, using a rifle approach, not some broad-brush approach, is really what we're able to deliver, and sponsors are associated with the alternative programming that we bring, which are specially important. They help make the product available but they also provide extra revenue screens for us, and we do that and pre-show advertising now which is more the traditional captive way we take, we see this going to another level entirely.

Interviewer: So, let me ask you because you have so much experience in this business. You came across a challenge in this business, you solved it, you rectified it and you jumped on the future. What does the future look like from here?

Interviewee: The future is building a media company that's what we think of ourselves as, the platform for that media company, our theaters around the country in the top DMAs. So we can deliver to a content owner and a sponsor the markets and the audiences they're interested in.

5）变化与拓展

    小组讨论通常适合较为不熟悉的、需要深入讨论的话题，而且花费的时间较长。教师和学生之间的问答是一种更为简便的激活背景知识的方法，也便于教师把控方向。教师可以从自身的经历、他人的事例或者社会热点，非常自然地引入话题，与学生展开问答。

每个人的知识面都存在个体差别。一个人回答得不全面的话，可以再问一个人，所以师生问答实际上是采用全班共享的形式来激活背景知识。

教师可以提醒学生，激活背景知识实际上可被视为一种学习策略，用来帮助实现预测、联想、推断等认知策略，以及计划、监督等元认知策略。在自主听力活动中，也应在听前通过标题、任务、情境等各种方式激活背景知识。

2.4.5 理解型听力活动设计五：拓展工作记忆

1）要点讲解

听写是常见的听力练习形式。在一定程度上，它也能帮助拓展短时语音记忆。在听写时，大脑必须在工作记忆中保持住词汇或句子的语音序列，直到词汇或句子被写下来为止。听写的内容可按照训练阶段的不同，从单词到词组，再到短句，再到长句。也可以练习听写非词及其序列。非词是研究者利用某种语言的基本音素、模仿其发音规则制造出来但是没有意义的假词。例如，英语非词可以是 chut、gern、barp，等等。心理学家利用非词重复或者非词序列回忆来测试一个人的工作记忆容量，教师也可以用它们做专门的短时语音记忆训练。

例如，教师将用不同次序排列的非词读出来，比如第一个是 chut、barp、gern，第二个是 barp、chut、gern，请学生判断听到的这两个三词序列是否相同。判断两个三词序列的单音节非词是比较简单的。增加序列里的非词数量到四词、五词和六词，就能增加任务的难度。这样的练习也可拓展短时记忆容量。

另一个拓展语音记忆的方法是跟读。可以在听的过程中随时暂停所听材料，要求学生立刻口头重复刚才听到的句子。后续的练习可以通过逐渐增加句子长度，达到拓展工作记忆的目的。

2）课前准备

（1）选取一段语速偏快的听力材料，制成听写练习。如果是单词填空练习，空与空之间应保留适当的距离，以便学生书写。如果是听写长句，则采用按暂停键的办法，给学生足够的时间书写。

（2）制作若干个非词，单音节和多音节均可。可将其制成三词组、四词组和五词组，每组可排列成不同序列，如上例中 chut、gern、barp 可有 1) chut、gern、barp；2) chut、barp、gern；3) barp、gern、chut；4) barp、chut、gern；5) gern、barp、chut；6) gern、chut、barp 等六种不同序列。这是三个词的序列，还可制作四词和五词一组的序列供练习。

3）活动实例

听前

本次练习采用的听力材料是一篇研究灵长类动物个性的文章。文中有不少生词，单音节、双音节和多音节（3 个音节及以上）的生词都有。在听之前，教师介绍这次听力任务是：听生词，记住其发音。本例中选取了 mesh、option、species、intriguing、neuroticism、conscientiousness、primatology 等七个生词。为熟悉规则，教师先用 interesting 这个词做示范，要求学生在听一遍单词之后说出这个词；再用一个非词 charlembeet 做例子，要求学生复述并强调要记住音节的次序。

听中

教师播放一遍生词的音频，随即要求学生复述每个单词，然后做别的事情，如讨论有关动物的话题。5 分钟后要求学生再复述一遍每个单词。此练习的目的是锻炼学生的语音记忆，拓展他们记忆语音序列的能力。词汇的意思和拼写不是记忆的重点。

听后

教师讲解语音记忆的知识，用课前准备的非词序列给学生做记忆小测试，让学生听三词序列、四词序列和五词序列的对子，判断听到的对子是否次序相同。例如，教师先说出 chut、gern、barp、doop，再说出 chut、barp、gern、doop，学生应判断出两次听到的次序是不同的。

4）音视频文本

Human personalities, as is widely agreed by psychologists, can be measured along five dimensions: extroversion, agreeableness, conscientiousness, neuroticism and openness to experience.

One person may be more extrovert than another, less agreeable, more conscientious and so on, and to an extent how well two people will get on can be predicted from how their personalities mesh.

People who don't get on, though, have the option of avoiding each other. That is not true of animals in zoos. But they too have personalities. So, to prevent trouble between members of one species – the chimpanzee – Hani Freeman of Lincoln Park Zoo in Chicago, has developed a way of assessing those personalities. In doing so, she sheds an intriguing light not only on chimpanzee psychology, but also on the mental evolution of Homo sapiens. As they reported in the *American Journal of Primatology*, Dr. Freeman and her colleagues started by surveying the existing literature on chimpanzee behavior.

5）变化与拓展

训练短时记忆的方法除了用生词、非词来做，还可用句子填空的形式。让学生听一篇短文，完成划线部分填空。划线部分要填写的是句子或句子片段。教师在每个划线部分结束时按暂停键，留足时间让学生回忆刚才记住的语音片段并写下来。例如：

Human personalities, <u>as is widely agreed by psychologists</u>, can be measured along five dimensions: extroversion, agreeableness, conscientiousness, neuroticism and openness to experience.

<u>One person may be more extrovert than another</u>, less agreeable, more conscientious and so on, and to an extent how well two people will get on can be predicted from how their personalities mesh.

上面这个练习也可以转变为跟读，即教师暂停后要求学生口头重复刚才听到的句子。

在设计句子（或句子片段）填空时，如果上下文中有相同的词或者同族词汇，不必完全回避，可以视之为减少难度的辅助，因为要学生聆听的是比较长的句子，而不是单个词汇。这一点不同于作为测试的听写题。

2.4.6　理解型听力活动设计六：开展合作听力

1）要点讲解

合作听力的一大好处是实现了听者之间的互动。互动与二语习得有密切的关系（Gass & Mackey 2015）。互动假设认为，当双方交流中出现问题时，就会产生更多的输入和反馈，有利于二语习得。其中，意义协商是学习者理解第二语言和发展二语能力的驱动力（Long 1996）。大量实证研究通过观察意义协商（如确认、核对、澄清）、形式协商（如纠错反馈）、语言相关片段（LREs）的数量，发现了互动的总体效果及其影响因素（Gass et al. 2005；Loewen 2005；汪清 2011）。但是，听力课堂基本上都是单向听力活动，并不能完全模拟真实交流环境，因此无法实现听者和说话人之间的这种互动。前文也已经提到，在传统的课堂上常常是学生先自己听，再做题，然后教师核对答案。这种方法重在检查听力理解的结果是否正确，却无法令师生双方关注到听力过程中遇到的具体问题和困难发生的具体原因，而合作听力可通过听者之间的互动在这一方面加以弥补。研究表明，合作听力活动使听者有机会相互协商听的内容，比照双方的理解过程，发现自己的薄弱环节，并促使自己在重复聆听中施加注意。总之，合作听力能够带来意义协商和形式协商，有利于促进二语学习者的语言理解和语言发展（王艳 2019）。

那么，合作听力活动与传统听力活动中的对子和小组讨论有什么不同？传统听力活动中的讨论，其目的是得出结果，而合作听力的目的是剖析过程。在听完第一遍之后，学生在对子和小组中核对自己尚不明确的理解，询问同伴的推理逻辑，交流听力过程中的疑难，这样在第二遍听的时候，就知道应在何处施加更多的注意。听完第二遍后，再次一起交流双方的理解，验证假设，评价理解过程中所使用的听力策略或方法的得失，双方或多方一起决定是否需要再听，以及如何完成具体任务，等等。

2）课前准备

（1）准备学生在合作聆听时常常需要用到的交际话语的英文表达。学生在与同伴的合作听力活动中，需要询问自己的理解是否正确、核实是否听到某个词、询问对方这样推理或判断的原因、述说自己的推理并希望对方评价、询问对方有没有难点等，对这些句子的英文表达，许多学生常常不够熟练，可集中学一学。例如：

- Is my understanding correct?
- Did you hear the speaker say… or…?
- Why do you think so?
- How do you know that?
- Could you give me any reasons?
- I guess that…because I heard…What do you think?
- I have difficulties in… What difficulties do you have when you listen?

（2）在合作听力中起到重要作用的是合作伙伴。随机组合是常用的方法，但是随机并不是意味着随意。应提前准备好抽签的纸条或者电脑分组小程序，方便在课堂上做随机抽取。如果教师希望按照水平、个性或者性别等属性把学生分成合适的对子或小组，就需要提前按所需属性分好组，再进行随机抽取。

3）活动实例

听前

这一篇听力材料的主题是社交平台的过度分享，涉及的是在朋友圈发文字、晒图等社交行为。话题有较强的时代感，与学生的生活体验非常贴近。但是，为体现评价的客观性，材料中引用了不同的学术观点，逻辑比较严密，乍一听有点弯弯绕。为了理解好这一篇，教师决定采用合作听力的活动方式，让学生结成 3 人小组，一起合作聆听并完成任务。各小组可以自主决定听几遍，在什么地方暂停，在什么地方重复，最后共同给出问题的答案。因为是第一次做合作听力活动，教师在开始前做了讲解和演示，以防学生把这项活动和一般的讨论活动相混淆。本例中，教师建议学生采用以下步骤：

- 在听前先浏览任务中的问答题，做好计划。
- 第一遍完整地听，不要暂停或重复。
- 听完第一遍之后即刻开始围绕问答题展开讨论，在遇到不一致观点时放慢讨论节奏，细致询问对方的理解过程。可参看屏幕上的询问方式来提问和回答（见上文的课前准备）。
- 在听第二遍或第三遍时，可在需要的地方暂停或重复。

听中

本例中，教师提前准备的讨论题如下：

- From a traditional perspective, is it good to share?
- According to the report, what is sadfishing? Is it negative or positive?
- What does Dr. Hand's research suggest?
- According to the report, we should steer clear of showing off, bragging or flexing. How do you understand the sentence? Do you agree or disagree with this claim? Give your reasons.

在讨论中，教师在各组间巡视，确保合作的有序进行，并时而参与讨论。一位学生表示，根据自己使用社交平台的经验，一开始就推测材料中会说 oversharing 是不好的，但是在听到 "…this form of oversharing could come from a strong desire to connect with someone" 和 "…the more we post on a platform, the more socially attractive we become" 的时候，反而觉得信息矛盾了。她询问同伴是怎么理解的，这一篇到底想表达什么。同伴表示也有疑惑，但是从材料最后部分推断出，主旨应该还是指人们应避免在社交平台吹嘘、夸大或博取同情。另一位学生说自己听到了 positive 和 negative 这两个词，认为材料的主旨是在社交平台应传递积极正面的东西。他们的第一次讨论虽然没有完全解决信息为何"矛盾"，但是三人决定在第二次听的时候重点注意那两处。最后，经过暂停、再听，三人完全弄懂了，原来几处看似不一致的观点来自材料中对不同专业人士话语的引用。

听后

各组活动完成后，教师先请学生发言，再做进一步总结。教师借上述例子说明，引用各方观点是为了显示客观，从多个角度看问题，在不够确定的问题上避免过激看法。同时，教师又举出文中几处使用模糊限制语的句子，询问学生是否注意到 seem、generally，以及 could、would 等情态动词，并举例如下：

- This could be due to a belief that we attract our own negative experiences the more we share them.
- It seems that sadfishing, the idea of searching for sympathy by oversharing, is generally perceived as negative rather than the cry for help it could actually be.
- However, Dr. Hand's research also seems to suggest that the more we post on a platform, the more socially attractive we become – provided that the posts we bang out are positive.
- They would probably be more than happy to tell you if your posts about your breakfast or your gripes about your lack of money really are too much.

4）音视频文本

It's good to share, right? Growing up as kids we are told to share our toys and not be selfish. We also live in an age where discussing our feelings is encouraged. But when does it all become too much? With new crazes trending all the time, such as dance challenges and wearing a pillow as a dress, the question is: When has sharing become oversharing on social media?

What is oversharing? The term has become associated with social media, but it isn't exclusive to this platform. Imagine you head to a party and you meet someone. Within five minutes they have divulged intimate details about their life. While some of us may try to escape these people, according to marriage therapist Carolyn Cole, this form of oversharing could come from a strong desire to connect with someone. But how does this translate to social media?

Dr. Christopher Hand, a lecturer in cyberpsychology, says the more details people disclose, the less sympathy we express when things go wrong. This could be due to a belief that we attract our own negative experiences the more we share them.

It seems that sadfishing, the idea of searching for sympathy by oversharing, is generally perceived as negative rather than the cry for help it could actually be. However, Dr. Hand's research also seems to suggest that the more we post on a platform, the more socially attractive we become – provided that the posts we bang out are positive. Even back in 2015, Gwendolyn Seidman, said that we should avoid whining and being negative online. We should also steer clear of showing off, bragging or flexing, as it's now known – especially about our love lives. It makes sense – if your date is going "that well", would you really have time to share a photo with text?

So, how can you know if you are oversharing? Well, why not ask your friends in real life? They would probably be more than happy to tell you if your posts about your breakfast or your gripes about your lack of money really are too much.

5）变化与拓展

合作听力活动可以从人数、同伴和组间联系等方面变化出不同的方式。人数上，可以根据听力任务的时长、难度和重要性（是主要课文还是辅助材料）等来决定是同桌之间展开合作，还是前后座位形成3—4人组，或者形成5—6人的大组。为让学生接触不同的合作方，教师还可以时常更换学生合作活动的同伴，这就需要增加抽签等环节。小组形成之后，一般是组内活动居多，但是教师如能有条理地组织好组间的交流（如组间相互评价），就能够更好地提高全体学生的参与度。教师应寻找恰当的时机加入到小组中去，成为临时合作成员，既可以观察和发现问题，也可以提供引导和反馈。值得注意的是，语音室的设备限制（座位隔间和耳机线），往往对小组活动有些阻碍。教师也应提前考虑这些因素。

第三章　思辨听力活动

3.1　思辨听力的情境案例

在思辨听力的第一堂课，我曾经问过学生们什么是思辨。有的说思辨就是多角度看问题，有的说思辨就是质疑，也有的指出思辨是为了决策。尽管说得不够全面，但是可以看出大家都知道思辨是一种重要的能力。对于如何提高这种能力，特别是如何在听力课上实现思辨，学生们既感到好奇，也有些茫然。

我使用的听力教材里有专门的思辨听力练习，既有基于材料的题目，也有完全开放的题目。有一篇对话谈论的是一所海外知名大学，听完后要求学生回答三道思辨问题。最后一题是这样的：请问你自己有怎样的评价大学的标准？如果按照你自己的标准，该怎样评价所听材料中提到的这所大学？这是一道典型的开放式题目。我认为，学生经过思考，应该在对大学的评价方面有自己的想法。所以，我预想这个答案应该是比较丰富和有个性的。

然而，事实出乎意料。学生们的回答相当一致，就是听力材料中提到的这所大学的一些特点。是什么导致他们的回答与文中说话人的表述如此雷同？是受到听力材料中说话人观点的影响吗？是因为习惯了照文中意思来回答问题从而避免犯错？还是一时不知道怎么用英文说，就直接借用文中的表达来完成任务？或者还是不愿意独立思考？我该怎样启发他们养成批判性思考的习惯？

思辨听力（Critical Listening）是指在听的过程中运用恰当的评价标准，进行有意识的思考，最终做出有理据的判断（Paul & Elder 2006；文秋芳等 2009；王艳 2015）。思辨听力是思辨能力在听力活动中的运用和体现。本章将先简单阐述思辨能力的重要性和思辨听力教学的必要性，在此基础上介绍思辨听力的教学目标，然后讲解如何设计课堂教学来实现这些目标，最后是教学案例。

3.2　思辨听力的理论框架

3.2.1　思辨能力

思辨（Critical Thinking），又常常被译为批判性思维。批判性思维，从字面上容易被误解为对人或事进行"批判"，而实际上它是指一种理性的、反思性的思维。为避免这一误解，文秋芳等（2009）曾撰文提出采用"思辨"一词来表达这一短语，本书也采用这一表达。思辨的过程是分析和评价思维的过程（Paul & Elder 2006），因此思辨能力实际上是一种高层级思维能力，是关于思考的思考，是依据标准对事物或看法做出有目的、有理据的判断的能力。思辨能力既包括认知技能，也包括情感特质；思辨过程还包括元认知，即对自己的思维过程进行管理与监控（文秋芳等 2009）。

思辨能力被各国高等教育部门视为重要的人文性目标，是适应未来社会发展的人才所必备的能力。我国 2018 年颁布的《国标》也已经将思辨能力纳入其中，这体现了新的历史背景下国家和社会对外语专业人才培养的要求。实际上，从外语专业学生"思辨缺席症"的讨论（黄源深 1998；文秋芳、周燕 2006）到思辨能力的界定和测量（文秋芳等 2009，2010），再到倡导以思辨能力为导向，推进高校外语教学改革（孙有中 2011，2017；孙有中等 2011），中国外语界对思辨能力的研究已经持续了 20 多年。思辨能力是外语人才培养的关键能力之一，这一点已经达成共识。

3.2.2　思辨听力

Critical Listening（思辨听力或批判性倾听）这一术语在不同领域有不同含义，听的对象可以是音乐，也可以是语言。在音乐教育领域，批判性倾听是指对音乐要素的感知、识别、分析与评价（如 Smialek & Boburka 2006）。在教育学、管理学和医学护理等领域，批判性倾听的对象则是语言。在教育学领域，早在 20 世纪 40 年代到 80 年代，欧美中小学教育研究中（如 Duker 1962；Lundsteen 1966）就出现了对批判性倾听的研究。其中，Lundsteen（1966）所定义的 Critical Listening 包含以下四个方面：

（1）按照相关的客观证据考察听力材料；

（2）将所评价的观点与某些标准相比较；

（3）对此观点做出判断；

（4）对所做的判断施以行动。

可见，欧美国家比较早就开始关注思辨在语言学习中的作用，培养学生在听的时候进行思辨。我们知道，位列人们日常语言活动第一位的就是"听"。中小学生每天坐在教室里听老师讲课，大学生也要花大量的时间听讲座、参加研讨。在 20 世纪 90 年代之后，听力越来越受到重视。Wolvin & Coakley（1994）提出听力能力（Listening Competence）的概念。为了提高听的能力，许多大学在交流学课程中开设母语听力课程，其中差不多一半的时间用来教批判性倾听，在教材中也有独立的章节（Lucas 2008；Beebe & Beebe 2009）。例如，Beebe & Beebe（2009：40）在公共演讲课教材中的第五章，专门谈到如何去听。他们给出的定义是，批判性倾听就是通过听去评价所听信息的质量、恰当性、价值和重要性。

值得注意的是，这些课程是对母语学习者开设的听力课程。其目的显然不在于语言理解，而是在于提高他们的听力思辨能力。这一点，从美国交流协会提出的听力能力标准（NCA 1998）和 Wolvin & Coakley（1994）的研究就可以看出。这一标准包括：识别主要观点和具体细节；识别关系；回忆主要观点和细节；用开放的心态去注意、发现偏见；发现语言与非语言行为的不一致之处，等等。这里体现了不少思辨的特征。

那么，是否需要发展外语学习者的听力思辨？

培养外语学习者的听力思辨能力，同样具有非常重要的意义。作为学外语的学生，外语听得如何呢？是否有过这样的经历：听外语讲座，只觉得都听懂了，但当结束时讲座人问有什么问题，却忽然觉得没有头绪，不知从何处发问。即使能问个一二，也感觉没有深度。这正是黄源深（1998）最早提出"思辨缺席"时所指出的现象。如果不能对所听到的内容做出分析、推断与评价，那么即使都听懂了，也只能停留在理解的层面，而无法再进一步，提出所谓的"有质量"的问题。相反，如果在听的过程中，能够就内容的准确性、清晰度、深度、广度、正当性、可靠性等做出思考和评价，那么提出有价值的问题几乎是顺理成章的事情。

听力思辨的不足通常不易被发觉。学生思辨能力的缺乏，比较容易表现在"说"和"写"的方面，如在口头表达时，说理却缺乏"辩"的过程，或者在写作时缺乏"逻辑思维"（孙有中等 2011）。然而，我们不难推断，输入过程的思辨不足会导致输出过程中的思辨不足。一个人如果不会批判地去听，只习惯于人云亦云，那么自然提不出有质量的问题。可见，听力思辨能力会影响表达的深度。可以说，听力思辨能力决定着学习者对口头语言的处理质量，也会影响其他语言活动的质量。因此，思辨听力的学习非常必要。

3.2.3　思辨能力的理论模型

要清楚了解思辨能力的内涵，必须深入理解 Bloom 等（1956）和 Anderson & Krathwohl（2001）提出的认知分层理论、Paul & Elder（2006）的三元结构模型以及文秋芳等（2009）的层级模型。这些理论及模型为思辨听力教学提供了理论框架。

1）认知分层理论

Bloom 等（1956）首先提出认知分层理论，将人类的学习行为做了分级。几十年后，Anderson & Krathwohl（2001）根据该领域新的研究成果对层级做了修订。从记忆、理解，到运用、分析，再到评价和创造，认知分层理论体现了由简单到复杂的认知技能分类，如图 3.1 所示。这一理论说明了基础思维能力和高阶思维能力的关系。以理解为目标的听力是基础思维能力，以思辨为目标的听力是高阶思维能力。

图 3.1：认知分层理论 (修订版)

2) 三元结构模型

Paul & Elder（2006）认为，思维包含基本的思维要素、思维标准和思维特质。思维要素（Elements of Thought）有八项，包括目的（purpose）、问题（question at issue）、信息（information）、推断（interpretation and inference）、概念（concepts）、假设（assumptions）、蕴意（implications and consequences）和观点（point of view）（如图 3.2 所示）。衡量上述思维要素的标准包括清晰性、准确性、精确性、相关性、深刻性、广阔性、完整性、逻辑性、重要性和公正性。Paul & Elder（2006）还提出了八项思辨特质，包括谦虚、独立、诚实、勇气、毅力、相信理性、同理心和公正。

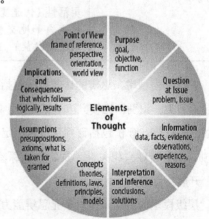

图 3.2：思维要素 (Paul & Elder 2006：9)

3）层级模型

为了突出思辨者的主观能动性在思辨能力中的主导作用，文秋芳等（2009）提出的层级模型引进了元思辨能力的概念。它位于第一层次，在第二层次思辨能力（包括认知技能、认知标准、情感特质）之上，对第二层次起到管理与监控作用。

表 3.1：文秋芳等（2009）的层级模型

元思辨能力（自我调控能力）——第一层次		
思辨能力——第二层次		
认知		情感
技能	标准	好奇（好疑、好问、好学） ------------------
分析（归类、识别、比较、澄清、区分、阐释等） ------------------ 推理（质疑、假设、推论、阐述、论证等） ------------------ 评价（评判预设、假定、论点、论据、结论等）	精晰性（清晰、精确） ------------------ 相关性（切题、详略得当、主次分明） ------------------ 逻辑性（条理清楚、说理有根有据） ------------------ 深刻性（有广度与深度） ------------------ 灵活性（快速变化角度、娴熟自如地交替使用不同思辨技能）	开放（宽忍、尊重不同意见，乐于修正自己的不当观点） ------------------ 自信（相信自己的判断能力、敢于挑战权威） ------------------ 正直（追求真理、主张正义） ------------------ 坚毅（有决心、毅力，不轻易放弃）

在这一模型中，思辨的认知技能包括分析、推理和评价等三项。其中，分析包括归类、识别、比较、澄清、区分、阐释等；推理包括质疑、假设、推论、阐述、论证等；评价包括评判预设、假定、论点、论据、结论等。认知标准有五项，即精晰性、相关性、逻辑性、深刻性和灵活性。五条情感特质包括好奇、开放、自信、正直和坚毅。

层级模型的特点是提出了元思辨能力。元思辨能力在思辨听力中有重要的作用。它是一种自我调节能力，起到对思辨的计划、监控、调整与评估的作用。

3.2.4　二语思辨听力的认知框架

笔者曾根据"德尔斐"项目组（the Delphi Project）的双维模型和文秋芳等（2009）的层级模型，提出二语思辨听力的认知框架（王艳 2015），指出了二语思辨听力应包含的认知技能，参见图 3.3。该框架从三个方面加以考虑：第一，二语思辨听力应突出思辨的核心技能，所以该模型保留了"德尔斐"项目组提出的四项思辨能力的核心技能，即"阐释""分析""评价""推理"（Facione 1990）；第二，二语思辨听力离不开听力过程的基本认知特点，因此笔者加入"感知"和"理解"这两种技能（Brownell 2010；Dwyer et al. 2014）。从"感知"和"理解"，到"阐释""分析""评价""推理"，是一个从基础技能到高级技能的过程；第三，笔者认为思辨听力有明确的目的和解决问题的倾向，听者需要有高层次的认知活动来协调所有的认知过程。因此，该框架借鉴文秋芳等（2009）的层级模型，将自我调节能力视为重要的元思辨能力，在思辨过程中起到计划、检查、调整与评估的作用。

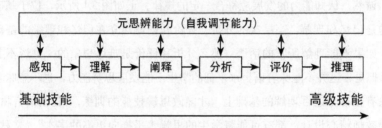

图 3.3　二语思辨听力的认知框架（王艳 2015）

每种技能包含的多个分技能如下：

感知：听辨语音、有选择地施加注意、感知非语言信号；

理解：切分语音流、识别词汇、理解话语意思；

阐释：归类、理解意义、澄清意思；

分析：分析看法、找出论据、分析论证过程；

评价：评价观点、评价论据；

推理：质疑证据、提出替代假设、得出结论；

自我调节：自我评估、自我纠正。

3.3　思辨听力的教学目标

思辨听力教学在我国高校听力教学领域中尚属新生事物。因此，以下思辨听力教学目标的前两条更侧重于阐释思辨听力总的教学原则，后两条是具体阐释如何从思维要素的识别与评价出发来实现教学目标。

3.3.1　以语言理解为基础，发展高层次思维能力

思辨既是一种技能，也是一种习惯，它并不局限于学科或内容（Scriven & Paul 2008）。听力的思辨，和说、读、写过程中需要培养的思辨能力有同样的本质。前面提到过对母语听力思辨的教学，但是二语听力思辨能力的培养与之相比有明显的难度。的确，很多外语学习者在听力课堂上急需解决的是语言理解的问题，还无暇顾及批判性思考。那么，是不是听力水平低的学生就无法发展思辨能力，或者说如果对听力材料没有完全理解，就没有办法思辨？

诚然，认知能力的发展应符合一定的规律。正如图 3.1 所示，位于基础层次的是记忆和理解，高层次的分析、评价和创造建立在记忆和理解的基础之上。如果不能理解所听的话语，那么分析和评价是难以想象的，更谈不上创造。但是，这并不意味着语言水平低的学生不能发展思辨能力，也不意味着我们只有在百分之百理解的基础上，才能做思辨技能的训练。"任何语言材料，只要教师精心设计，都有可能将学生的思辨水平推向更高的层次"（文秋芳、孙旻 2015）。在确定思辨听力教学目标的时候，我们既要做到循序渐进，夯实基础，也要做到将高层次思维活动细化、分解，与基本技能相关联。具体地说，我们可以将以理解为目标的教学置于思辨听力活动之前，为高层次思维活动扫清障碍；同时，也可以在基础任务上合理延伸，把思辨技能融入进去。

3.3.2　以认知技能为重点，兼顾情感特质的发展

在重点训练认知技能的同时，教学还应兼顾思辨听力的情感特质发展。思辨听力过程中所涉及的情感，与在其他思辨过程中所涉及的情感并无二致。但

是，由于听力过程本身的特点，思辨听力尤其需要培养好奇、自信、坚毅等情感。听力活动以输入为主，只有养成喜欢质疑、喜欢刨根问底的习惯，才能改变不假思索、全盘接受的思维定式。听力过程中的压力和焦虑感普遍大于其他类型的学习活动，在这样的情况下要做到思辨，考验的是听者的自信和坚毅。自信是学习者相信自己的判断力，敢于挑战权威；坚毅使学习者百折不挠，通过多次努力达到目标。可以说，情感特质能够促进认知技能的发展，而锻炼认知技能的同时，情感特质也能够得到培养。认知技能和情感特质是相辅相成、相互促进的关系。

3.3.3　识别听力材料中的思维要素

　　实施思辨听力教学的方法是多种多样的。教师可以根据学生的情况和所用的教材，具体设计教学方案。本章介绍的是基于 Paul & Elder（2006）的框架，从思维要素和思维评价标准入手来设计思辨听力的教案。思维的八个要素包括目的、问题、信息、推断、概念、假设、蕴意和观点。下面以日常会话、讲座和新闻等三个听力体裁为例简要介绍。

　　日常会话的目的，或是朋友寒暄，或是互通信息；讲座的目的通常是传递知识，激发学术思考；新闻的目的则通常是报道最新消息，引发听众关注。日常会话可能涉及一个或几个话题，讲座有讲座的主题，新闻报道也是如此。无论是哪种体裁，都会以主题为中心来组织信息。日常会话中，说话人会从自己的体验、知道的信息出发，可能会运用与听者相同或不同的假设，可能传达与听者所持有的相同或不同的观点。在讲座中，讲座人会聚焦于明确的问题，利用数据、事实、观察、体验等主客观信息，通过推理来阐明概念、检验假设，还常常会涉及问题带来的相关启示。可见，如果从目的、问题、信息、推断、概念、假设、蕴意、观点等思维要素的角度来分析会话和讲座，就不会仅仅停留于对它们意思的理解。同样地，听新闻报道的时候，如果以思辨为目标，那么我们就不会只满足于听出"时间""地点""人物"和"事件"了，还会就新闻报道的目的、所提出的问题、所依据的证据、所传达的观点和意义以及推理的过程等做出批判性的思考。

Paul & Elder（2006）的思维要素框架使思辨听力教学活动变得更容易操作。第一步是识别思维要素。在教学中，为了解学生是否识别了听力材料中的思维要素，通常可使用如下问题进行提问：

- What is the purpose?
- What are the questions/problems/issues?
- What information is used?
- What concepts are utilized?
- What inferences are made?
- What assumptions are based on?
- What are the implications/consequences?
- What is the speaker's point of view?

3.3.4 评价听力材料中的思维要素

第二步是对思维要素进行评价。思维要素的评价标准，可以采用前面所述的 Paul & Elder（2006）的 10 条标准，也可以采用文秋芳等（2009）精简的 5 条标准，即精晰性、相关性、逻辑性、深刻性、灵活性。例如，可以评价所听材料的理据是否精确、论证过程是否清晰、与话题是否相关、看问题的角度是否全面、是否有深度，等等。以下这些问题可用来引导评价。

- Is the problem explained clearly?
- Is this a significant issue?
- What is the source of the statistics?
- Is the source reliable?
- What is the speaker taking for granted?
- Are these assumptions justifiable?
- Are they consistent?
- On what basis are the inferences made?
- Are they justified?
- Are they logical?

　　运用思维要素框架，结合教材的具体内容，我们还可以设计出思辨听力课程单元的具体目标。例如：

- interpret the meaning of education from various perspectives;
- identify the different assumptions on parenting;
- evaluate the statistical evidence of facts about world population;
- compare and evaluate different versions of explanation for global warming;
- evaluate the consequences of Columbus' discovery of the New World;
- generate implications of wildlife protection.

（选自《大学思辨英语教程视听说》第 1 册）

3.4　思辨听力教学设计实例

　　这一部分针对八个要素分别设计了教学活动。每个教学活动含有要点讲解、课前准备、活动实例、音视频文本和变化与拓展等五个部分。

3.4.1　思辨听力活动设计一：识别和评价"目的"

1）要点讲解

　　人们的交流是有目的的。问候朋友、传递信息、说明自己的观点……这是我们日常聊天说话的目的；商品销售员描述产品的种种优点，目的是劝说我们购买产品；新闻告诉我们世界上发生了什么；专家、学者或者教师通过讲座向听众传递知识；短视频里的博主分享他们旅行的见闻；各种听书平台上的小说连载、电视里播放的相声和小品等则是兼具休闲和娱乐的目的。

　　思维也如同交流一样，不会漫无目的。Paul & Elder（2006）认为："人类的思维与他的目标、期望、需求和价值观是相一致的。我们要了解自己和他人的思维，首先要了解它的目的、方向、内容和功能。"然而，很多人并不十分清楚自己思维的目的，也没有弄清对方思维的目的。不知道自己思维的目的和方向，会导致自己思维效率的下降；如果与人交流，误解就时有发生。即便不至于误解，也会导致与他人交流效率的降低。怎样才能洞晓思维的目的？实际上，目的并非总是显而易见。人们有时会明讲，有时却会掩饰，还有很多时候前后不一致。

目的和视角是相互影响的。也就是说，目的会影响我们看问题的角度，同时又会受到视角的反作用。同样地，目的还会塑造我们看问题的方式，而我们看问题的方式也决定着我们最终能找寻到什么。在思辨听力中，如果我们聆听说话人说话的时候能了解他们的思维目的，那将有助于我们做出一系列判断，如评价他们是否存在偏见、评价他们的信息来源是否可靠、评价他们所使用的概念和数据是否准确、评价他们所说的话是否有意义，等等。

2）课前准备

（1）教师可准备不同目的的音视频材料，供学生分析比较。可包括：日常寒暄、机场航班播报、天气预报、法庭辩论、科学讲座、新闻报道、商业广告、电视购物、总统竞选辩论、美食制作等。

这些材料可以选自电影或电视剧片段，或者新闻网站、TED 演讲、短视频，或者是现场录音（如机场航班播报）。这些音视频可能具有单一的目的，也可能不止一个目的。音视频不必太长，1—3 分钟左右即可。备课中，教师需要准备好两组问题，第一组是有关"目的"的提问，第二组是有关评价的提问，用来引导对"目的"是否清晰、是否现实、是否与其他目的矛盾、是否合理、是否有意义等方面的评价。

（2）可以采用口头练习或书面练习。如果是书面练习，可以准备如下所示的连线题：左侧是音视频材料的编号，右侧是表示目的的动词。

- 材料 1   To persuade
- 材料 2   To inform
- 材料 3   To explain
- 材料 4   To instruct
- 材料 5   To describe
- 材料 6   To evaluate
- 材料 7   To entertain

3）活动实例

听前

教师采用课前准备的短视频（一则天气播报、一则广告、一条新闻和一场电视辩论），分别让学生说明它们的目的。听前，教师还可询问大家对海洋重要性的看法。

听中

本例是一个科普访谈节目。视频中几位海洋科学家在讨论海洋的生态。第一位是海洋生物学家 Sylvia Earle，她指出海洋是维持人类生命的系统。另两位科学家补充了事实和数据。但是，传递这些看法和信息是否就是他们的全部目的？显然不是。在视频的后半部分，他们指出，人类正在破坏海洋这个人类赖以生存的重要的生态系统。他们呼吁人们做出改变。所以，这一视频的主要目的是摆事实讲道理，劝说人们重视这一问题，并以切实的行动来改变现状。

教师设计了如下的选择题，在学生看完一遍视频后，将题目显示在屏幕上让学生回答。

Which of the following best describes the purpose of the speakers?

a) to instruct

b) to entertain

c) to describe

d) to persuade

在明确目的之后，教师引导大家对目的进行评价。视频播放第二遍，用来评价的问题（可参照前文提出的思辨要素的评价标准）如下：

• Is the purpose clear?

• Is it realistic?

• Is it contradictory to other goals?

• Is it justifiable?

• Is it fair?

听后

教师将文本显示在屏幕上，让学生找出其中哪些是事实，哪些是观点。本例中，三位受访者给出了很多事实和数据，但是里面也带有观点。区分清楚事实和观点，有助于明确目的。

4）音视频文本

Sylvia Earle:	Many people look at the ocean and they see water. It's not just water. It's alive.
Robert Ballard:	The largest mountain ranges on the planet are beneath the sea. The deepest canyons are beneath the sea.
Enric Sala:	The oceans give us more than half of the oxygen we breathe, regulate the climate, give us all the seafood and recreational opportunities.
Sylvia Earle:	It's our life support system.
	…
Sylvia Earle:	Every breath we take, every drop of water we drink, we are connected to nature, especially to the ocean.
Robert Ballard:	The oceans cover 71% of the planet.
Enric Sala:	12% of the land is protected in national parks or reserves. In the ocean, less than 1% is protected.
Robert Ballard:	We are sort of a little creature living on the back of this much larger creature, but we've now reached a point where we can actually do harm to our host. And I don't think people realize that their earth is so vulnerable.
Sylvia Earle:	We've lost 90% of the big fish in the sea; We've seen a decline of coral reefs and growth in the death zones.
Enric Sala:	People have the ability to make history, to create positive change. We need another revolution. We need a healthier planet.

5）变化与拓展

这个活动也可以用主观题的形式来提问，如 What is the purpose of the three speakers? 主观题能够给学生更多的表达空间，也能及时发现理解上的具体偏差。

当我们从不同的角度看待问题时，就会发现有时所听材料的目的不止一个，可引导学生判别最根本的目的，让他们给出判定的理由，同时允许不同观点的存在。思维八要素可以分开学习，也可以两三个一起学习。例如，这篇听力材料里面含有数据，提供了佐证观点的支撑信息，它们都是思辨的要素。为叙述方便，本文分开阐述，但是在实际教学中是可以综合在一起练习的。教师可根据听力材料的内容，决定侧重点。

评价的问题大多是开放的，听力材料中可能有也可能没有明确的依据，相关信息也不充分。这时需要学生利用自己已有的知识或者查询资料进行回答，言之有理即可。

3.4.2　思辨听力活动设计二：识别和评价"问题"

1）要点讲解

当我们进行批判性思维的时候，总要了解清楚我们需要解决的问题是什么。这是因为解决问题、达成目标，实际上决定了思维的方向。英文中的 question、problem 和 issue 这三个词，是在这里要讨论的关键词。这三个词意思相近，中文里"问题"既可能是 question，也可能是 problem，它既表示"要求回答的题目"，也表示要"加以解决的疑难"，而 issue 是指一个重大的、悬而未决的问题。三者的共同之处，是都需要讨论或解决。例如，在前一例海洋科学家的讨论中，要解决的具体问题是海洋的保护，而背后的重要问题是生态环保。不同的目的对应不同的问题。对以传递信息为目的的材料，我们回答的问题是"内容是什么"；对以解释原因或劝说为目的的材料，要回答的问题就是"为什么是这样的"或"为什么要这么做"；对以指导步骤为目的的材料，回答的问题就是"怎样去做"。在本例中，我们要指导学生听出材料中的 problem、question 和 issue，理解它们之间的区别与联系，并学会如何评价。

2）课前准备

教师可选择学术讲座、纪录片或著名演讲片段作为听力材料。材料应具备明确的重要问题（issue），若里面能体现需要解决的困难或问题（problem 或 question）则更好。在备课时，教师需要准备好两组问题，第一组问题是有关内容的，其中应包含对 problem、question 和 issue 的提问。例如：

- What question is the speaker trying to answer?
- What problem is the speaker trying to solve?
- What issue is the speaker discussing?

第二组是有关评价的提问，与前文所述类似，主要是评价问题的准确性、逻辑性、清晰度、深度、意义等，如所提的问题是否清楚？对该问题的解释是否到位？是否能够提得更加准确？这个问题是否过于简单或者复杂？这个问题是否有意义？它是有关哪个领域的重要问题？例如，政治、经济、文化、教育、科学、历史等领域。可提问如下：

- Is the question simple or complex?
- Is the problem explained clearly?
- What kind of problem is this? Political? Cultural? Educational? Scientific? Historical?
- Is this a significant issue?

3）活动实例

听前

怎样引导学生区别 problem、question 和 issue 呢？这里以一篇 TED 演讲为例。演讲人是一位高中学生，她在随父母去印度探亲的过程中，发现印度存在清洁饮用水供应不足的问题，继而萌生想法，想用自己所学的知识去解决这一问题。在这一例中，教师在听前就让学生对这三个词进行区别，再举例说明，目的是让学生将这三个容易混淆的词在意思和用法上先弄清楚。

听中

在观看视频 1—2 遍之后，教师提问以下的问题：

(1) Why do the speaker's parents always remind her to drink boiled or bottled water?

(2) Why do people stand in long lines under the hot sun to fill buckets with water from a tap?

(3) Why do children drink dirty water from streams on the roadside?

(4) What are the causes of this problem?

(5) What issue are we facing?

教师将学生组成 3—4 人小组，先在小组内讨论，然后在全班回答。教师对回答进行分析。第（1）题是对一个简单事实（父母提醒她喝瓶装水）背后原因的提问；第（2）—（3）题是演讲人在印度看到缺水现象时内心想问的问题，演讲人没有明说，但是听者根据语境可以推断出答案；第（4）题问的是这些现象的存在反映了什么问题（problem）。演讲人说到了 social injustice，即社会不公，她认为清洁水源并没有被公平地分配给每个人。接下来她指出，这反映了全球水资源危机的问题（We are facing a global water crisis）。这正回答了第（5）题所问的重要问题。演讲人使用了丰富的数据来支撑这一观点，同时也指出这一危机所带来的后果，即导致每天有 3000 名儿童死于与水资源污染相关的疾病（consequences 也是思维要素之一，详见思辨听力活动七）。

明确了 problem、question 和 issue 之后，教师提问前页的四个问题请学生逐一评价。这一演讲中提到的问题并不复杂，都反映了一个显而易见的事实，即演讲人所到之地的饮用水并不安全，人们需要排队来得到安全清洁的水，很多孩子甚至饮用不洁净的水。演讲人清楚地指出这是社会不公造成的，但是并没有进一步解释。众所周知，这一问题与经济、政治、文化等都有关系。它反映了全球水资源危机，具有极为重要的意义。

听后

教师总结识别和评价 problem、question 和 issue 的有效策略：要从细节理解出发，到整篇上把握主旨，同时也要调动自己的背景知识，把小的问题推至更宏观、更重大的问题去思考。

4）音视频文本

Every summer, my family and I travel across the world, 3,000 miles away to the culturally diverse country of India. Now, India is a country infamous for its scorching heat and humidity. For me, the only relief from this heat is to drink plenty of water. Now, while in India, my parents always remind me to only drink boiled or bottled water, because unlike here in America, where I can just turn on a tap and easily get clean, potable water, in India, the water is often contaminated. So my parents have to make sure that the water we drink is safe.

However, I soon realized that not everyone is fortunate enough to enjoy the clean water we did. Outside my grandparents' house in the busy streets of India, I saw people standing in long lines under the hot sun filling buckets with water from a tap. I even saw children, who looked the same age as me, filling up these clear plastic bottles with dirty water from streams on the roadside. Watching these kids forced to drink water that I felt was too dirty to touch changed my perspective on the world. This unacceptable social injustice compelled me to want to find a solution to our world's clean water problem. I wanted to know why these kids lacked water, a substance that is essential for life. And I learned that we are facing a global water crisis.

Now, this may seem surprising, as 75 percent of our planet is covered in water, but only 2.5 percent of that is freshwater, and less than one percent of Earth's freshwater supply is available for human consumption. With rising populations, industrial development and economic growth, our demand for clean water is increasing, yet our freshwater resources are rapidly depleting. According to the World Health Organization, 660 million people in our world lack access to a clean water source. Lack of access to clean water is a leading cause of death in children under the age of five in developing countries, and UNICEF estimates that 3,000 children die every day from a water-related disease.

5）变化与拓展

　　思辨类的活动，一般以提问和回答的形式为主。因为提问（特别是追问）往往能很好地追踪逻辑。提问的方式有多种，教师可直接提问，或待学生在对子或小组中讨论之后再提问，还可以让学生自由补充提问。对于评价，教师应多倾听不同学生的回答，并询问理由，最后给出总结。问题可以提前显示在屏幕上，让学生浏览，做好听前准备。如果教师为留有悬念，也可以不提前显示。

3.4.3　思辨听力活动设计三：识别和评价"信息"

1）要点讲解

　　要给出令人信服的观点，人们通常要依据事实、经验、数据等证据。在 Paul & Elder（2006）的思维要素框架中，这些统称为信息。在本活动中，思辨的核心任务是评价信息的真伪。说话人所认为的事实，是否确实属实？信息的来源是否可靠？说话人所依据的经验是否可能片面？或者带有偏见？

　　我们在交流中使用的信息，不可能都是亲身经历，它们当中有些来自媒体，有些来自他人转述；更何况即便是亲眼观察、亲身体验，也难免带有个人视角。因此，评价这些信息是否准确、清楚、相关，是否前后一致、是否有其他来源可以印证等，能够起到鉴别信息的作用。诚然，信息本来就难以做到百分之百的客观、公正和全面。但是思辨的过程，能够审视人类认知中可能存在的误差和信息传播中可能带来的扭曲。

2）课前准备

　　新闻报道常常需要提供相关的事实和数据，学术讲座则除了数据、图表和事实之外，还会带有演讲人的经验，这两类体裁都可以用来训练学生对信息的辨别和评价。同样地，教师在备课中要准备好提问。例如：

(1) What statistics are used in the news reports?

(2) What are the sources of the statistics?

(3) Are they reliable?

如果想就一个点来追问，还可以准备这样的问题：

(1) Does the speaker provide any information to answer the question?

(2) Is the information relevant?

(3) How do we know that this information is accurate?

(5) Do we need to gather more information?

3）活动实例

听前

本例是一则有关人口增长问题的新闻报道，文中有不少数据。教师的听前活动围绕数字的听读展开。英文里数字进位与中文里不同，比如 1 万是 10,000（ten thousand），十万是 100,000（one hundred thousand），70 亿是 7 billion。教师可用听读练习让学生熟悉规律并迅速反应。

听中

在听第一遍时，教师让学生把注意力放在新闻中使用的具体数据信息上，关注含有数字的句子并记录下来。文中有这样一些数据：

(1) There are already seven billion people living in this world.

(2) Half of the population is under the age of 25.

(3) We add almost a quarter of a million people a day to the planet every day.

(4) 222 million women worldwide who want to avoid or delay pregnancy have no access to birth control.

在听第二遍时，任务转为评价信息来源的可靠性、准确性等。新闻报道中的信息一般会指出来源，教师让学生们注意关键信息附近对新闻来源的交代，并将课前准备的问题显示在屏幕上，让学生在同桌间相互讨论。

这些数据是否真实可靠？第（1）条是基本常识，没有问题。需要提醒的是，数据在每天更新，该新闻报道发生在一段时间以前；第（2）条和第（3）条所提供的数据，虽然一般人并不太熟悉，但是可以核实。第（4）条信息，文中说明了来源，是来自联合国的报告。可以推断，这些数据基本上真实可靠。总体来说，这篇听力材料中的信息是清楚、准确和可靠的，与所报道的主题是相关的，有力地支撑了报道的主旨观点。但是，如果我们进一步阅读有关报告，了解其数据收集和分析方法，也许会发现统计上的瑕疵，据此我们就可提出质疑。教师指出，评价信息要有理有据，这个过程非常重要。不是听到什么就是什么。这就是在听力理解的基础上向前迈出思辨的一步。相比识别和判断信息本身，更为重要的是思辨态度和习惯的养成。

听后

教师展示听力材料的文本，提醒一些容易被忽略的信息点。它们可能不是数据形式，但是属于具体事实一类，如文中所举例的几位发展中国家女性的经历。这些信息同样需要识别和评价。

4）音视频文本

There are already seven billion people living in this world. Half of the population is under the age of 25. John Seager is president of Population Connection, an organization that promotes stabilizing population numbers.

"We add almost a quarter of a million people a day to the planet every day. And of course, the planet itself is not growing."

Seager says all women should be able to select the size of their families and, when they do, they typically choose to have fewer children.

But a recent United Nations report says 222 million women worldwide who want to avoid or delay pregnancy have no access to birth control. And the number of women not using contraception in the world's poorest countries has increased over the past four years.

Two of those countries are Pakistan and India. Ilhaam Jaffer came to the United States from Pakistan as an infant. Her mother is Pakistani and her father, Indian. She says talk of birth control in her parents' countries is often taboo for religious and cultural reasons.

"If a woman has a pregnancy prior to when she actually had plans on it, in her, you know, in her mind, like things like, you know, education and her career and like various other things are put on the back burner," Jaffer said.

Jaffer says that creates a society of young mothers with lower earning power and that ultimately affects the nation's economy.

Another poor country with a big population is Ethiopia. Mahala Dejene, arrived in the United States two years ago, says family planning has improved in Ethiopia.

"Before, you know, year by year, they have children. Now, they control their baby, you know, their family."

The United Nations calls for universal access to reproductive health by 2015. Ilhaam Jaffer thinks she knows the key to getting there. "The only solution I think is educating women, because if you educate a woman, you educate an entire family."

5）变化与拓展

教师还可以选择来自不同通讯社且有关同一事件的新闻报道来做听力练习。通过比较，可以发现信息来源的不同可能导致视角的不同。

对论据的识别，通常基于听力材料，而对论据的评价则相对开放，要判定的是学生的回答是否有理有据。课堂上无法判定的，鼓励学生课后查询资料，提供佐证，下一节课在课堂补充。

3.4.4　思辨听力活动设计四：识别和评价"推断"

1）要点讲解

推断是一件我们每天都要做无数次的事情。早上出门，看到天空布满乌云，你会推断今天可能会下雨；在下地铁的扶梯时，你看见前面的人快步走向站台，你会推断可能有地铁进站了；一向开朗话多的好朋友忽然不怎么说话了，你会推断她可能心情不好了。推断就是指我们依靠自己的观察、已有的知识或已知的前提得出结论的过程。

在听力材料中同样存在需要我们去推断的、没有明说的内容。通常，我们根据上下文线索，加上自己的知识和经验来推断句子中隐含的意思。换句话说，推断并不是胡乱做出的。它们是基于证据的、有理由的推理。值得注意的是，推断有的时候是基于信息，有的时候是基于假设。因此，推断可能是有理由的、符合逻辑的，也有可能并不是。气象台基于多年的数据做出天气预报，可信度比较高，但是"朋友不爱说话了就是心情不好"的假设未必准确，原因可能很多。事实上，人们并不总能意识到自己是在做推断，而且即便是意识到了，也总是认为自己思维正确、逻辑合理，推断出的就是事实。因此，作为一个听者，能够清楚地识别并合理地判断所听材料中的推断，是非常重要的。

2）课前准备

在各类听力材料中，都不难找到可以用来训练识别和评价"推断"的例子。教师需要深入分析材料，准备好引导学生识别和评价的问题，例如：

(1) What are the key inferences made in this lecture?

(2) On what basis are the inferences made?

(3) Are they justified?

(4) Are they logical?

3）活动实例

听前

教师给出一些情境，让学生做出推断，并相互评价。例如，读一篇短文或者播放一段影视剧对话，然后提问：What can we infer from the text? 或 What can we infer from the dialogue? 在一位同学回答之后，向另一位同学询问：Is his answer justified/logical? 用这些小练习让学生做推断，为下一步识别推断做好准备。

听中

本篇听力材料的主题是互联网，讲述的是蒂姆·伯纳斯·李（Tim Berners-Lee）在 1989 年提出将计算机联网的设想。在本篇听力材料中，我们听到 James Hendler，一位美国大学的教授，提到在美国已经有 80%—90% 的人连上互联网，覆盖率已经比较高，因此用户增长率反而不高，而中国的互联网用户的增长率为 25%，增长率比较高。他说他并不了解印度的数据，但是他做出推断，应该也是从较少的百分比开始，但是增长会很快。他的预测是基于中国和印度都是人口众多的国家这一共同点。

James Hendler 还推断说，互联网的潜力还远远没有被开发。他认为，人们对互联网背后的数学和工程学原理知道得较多，但是对互联网对社会的影响知之甚少。他这个推断是有其合理性的，因为通常一项新发明的社会影响比较深远，需要长时间才能显现。

推断的练习需要听者细细地梳理逻辑。在教学中，教师让学生听 1—2 遍，给学生充分的时间在两人对子或小组中进行讨论。讨论题如下：

(1) What did Tim Berners-Lee propose to do in 1989?

(2) What kind of growth did James Hendler, a professor from the Rensselaer Polytechnic Institute, think that India had in the development of the World Wide Web? On what basis did he make his inference?

(3) What did James Hendler think about the potential of the World Wide Web? Was his inference logical?

在讨论中，学生可以自主选择所需片段多次聆听。讨论之后，教师请学生发言，分析讲解。如果需要，教师还可以显示听力文本来分析。

听后

听者应区分清楚自己的推断和别人的推断。听者总是需要不断推断那些听力材料中没有明示的信息，这是听者自身的推断。实际上，推断正是常用的听力理解策略之一。而本课的思辨训练，是识别和评价材料中含有的推断。教师可根据前面活动中出现的问题，在听后进一步解释说明。

4）音视频文本

It all started in March of 1989. British scientist Tim Berners-Lee was working at CERN, the European Organization for Nuclear Research in Switzerland. Scientists would come to CERN from all over the world. But others could not see their research because of differences in computers.

Tim Berners-Lee thought it would be easier if all the computers could talk to one another and exchange information directly. So, he proposed linking the machines. His proposal would later become known as the World Wide Web.

It took two years before researchers could successfully link a computer server and web browser through the Internet. It would be officially launched in August 1991. By 1993, there would be more than 500 web servers. Now, there are more than 1.7 billion people on the Web worldwide.

"In the US, we are at somewhere between 80 and 90 percent of people already having access and, you know, not much growth. In China, you see about 25 percent and, of course, a country much bigger than ours. India, I don't know the current number, but again a small number growing very quickly. So, most of the growth we expect in the Web will actually be in those parts of the world that don't yet have it."

Twenty-five years after its invention, billions of people now use the World Wide Web. But James Hendler of the Rensselaer Polytechnic Institute says only a small part of the Web's potential has been realized.

"Here is this force that has really changed society in so many different ways. We understand sort of the mathematics of the computer network underneath it and the engineering of that, but we really don't understand the social impacts. There's more and more research that's starting to study what are those different effects. How do they affect society? How do we build the Web and keep it open and free? How do we really understand the impacts of this thing we call the World Wide Web?"

Tim Berners-Lee went on to create the World Wide Web Foundation. The group says in its mission statement that it wants to establish the open Web as a public good and a basic right.

5）变化与拓展

这一活动的拓展，可以是训练听者在识别和评价听力材料中含有的推断后，学会对自己所做出的推断有清晰的认知，应尽可能有理有据、符合逻辑。前文说过，课堂活动中思辨的对象是所听的材料。但是当活动完成之后，教师可拓展到听者对自身思维的反思。这是因为，当材料中信息不充分时，听者的识别和评价在很大程度上可能就是推断。拓展活动中提问的方式是类似的，但是对象变为自身的思维。

3.4.5 思辨听力活动设计五：识别和评价"概念"

1）要点讲解

人们在思考的时候都要用到概念。概念无处不在。思维与概念的关系非常紧密。没有概念，人们几乎无法思维。概念包括理论、定义、原理、模型等，它是思维的基本形式之一。概念反映客观事物的普遍的、本质的特征，可以用来表示物体、属性、（事物的）发生和过程，等等。概念用符号或词语来表示，它们是大脑中的表征，是抽象的物体或属性，它们是我们思维的基石。

"海洋""面积""时间""幸福""生活""勇敢"等，都是概念。当我们说"仁者乐山、智者乐水"的时候，这里的"山"和"水"都不是指任何一处具体的山和水，而是抽象的概念。当说到"狗"这个概念，我们一般是指那种四条腿、有皮毛和尾巴、被人们训练作为宠物或者帮助人们看家护院、完成导盲或缉毒工作的动物。当我们说，狗是人类的朋友时，我们并不是指任何一条具体的狗，而是将它作为一个抽象的概念。不同概念的抽象程度是不同的，"健康""速度""毕业"等是具体和熟悉的，而"社会性""女权主义""隐喻"等则是比较抽象的概念。

随着社会的发展，新的概念还在不断产生，如互联网、电子邮件、支付宝、低头族、云会议，等等。这些概念是不会为一百年前的人所理解的。随着新技术的发展，新的概念出现，新的词汇也就诞生了。这一点充分说明人类是使用词汇来形成概念的。我们利用概念来传递观点，在这个意义上也可以说，概念就是与词汇或符号相关联的、对观点或意义的表达。

概念在认知的各个领域发挥着重要作用，如分类、推断、记忆、决策，等等。在批判性思维方面训练有素的人，善于识别关键概念，并考察这些概念是否清楚、是否恰当、是否与主题相关以及如何解释它们，等等。识别和评价概念是听力思辨的重要一环。

2）课前准备

比较适合这一练习的听力材料是偏学术性的材料。这类听力材料含有较多术语及其定义或解释，以及帮助理解概念的例子。重点关注音视频材料中的关键概念，特别是那些容易理解偏差的概念和生僻的概念。可查找权威定义、补充实例，作为提供给学生的辅助资源。可制作问答题、填空题或者连线匹配题，来考查学生是否能准确听取概念并清楚了解它的含义。

对容易理解错误的概念，可以直接给出一对，引导学生区分和比较。例如：dimension/level、character/nature、aggressive/ambitious、passive/submissive、dominant/powerful 等。

3）活动实例

听前

教师采用思维导图，让学生围绕关键词，对将要听到的材料中的词汇做出预测。本例是一则讲述性别刻板印象的听力材料。这篇短文中最重要的概念有两个，即性别和刻板印象。以这两个词为中心主题，让学生发散性地思考其他有关联的词汇。

听中

让学生仔细聆听整个段落，边听边记下关键概念，听完后请他们说出对概念的理解，并评价这些概念是否清楚、是否恰当、是否与论题相关，等等。

性别是一个常见概念，其英文 gender 是对男性和女性的总称，但是这个词对于学习者来说，并不如 man、woman 或者 male、female 来得更为熟悉。Stereotype（刻板印象）是指人们对人或事物形成的一种固定的看法。这种看法常常过于简单或者片面，因此往往并不正确。这个概念比 gender 更为抽象。

这篇短文里还有其他概念。例如，在 "They tend to focus on four dimensions: character traits, roles in society, physical characteristics, and occupations" 这句中的维度、个性、社会角色、体形特征、职业等，都是概念。理解这几个基础概念有助于理解"性别刻板印象"这个关键概念。其实，整个短文本身就是对性别刻板印象的阐释。

听后

完成听力任务后，教师让学生回顾在听的时候是怎样理解关键概念的，有哪些困难，又有哪些技巧。教师介绍听力策略中的联想策略，即听者利用自己的已有知识以及听力材料中的语境线索来促进概念的理解和识别。

4）音视频文本

Gender stereotypes are generalized beliefs about people based on their genders. They tend to focus on four dimensions: character traits, roles in society, physical characteristics, and occupations. For example, whereas men are more likely to be considered as aggressive and competitive, women are more likely to be viewed as passive and cooperative. Traditionally, men have been viewed as bread-winners, whereas women have been viewed as caretakers. Physical characteristics and occupations have also been considered as being consistent or inconsistent with masculine or feminine roles. Traditional gender stereotypes are most representative of the dominant culture. They affect couple and family interactions. Often, for example, the division of household labor is based on gender. Traditionally, women in marriage remained at home and completed most of the domestic labor, while their male partners worked outside the home to provide the family income. Although women have increasingly joined the workforce over the past thirty years, they continue to do the majority of the household labor.

5）变化与拓展

给近义词是考查概念理解程度的另一个方法。解释一个概念需要下定义，这时近义词就非常有用。所以，听前和听中活动还可以采用匹配近义词、用近义词复述所听内容等练习。需要注意的是，听力材料中的概念会有很多，应抓住关键概念和重点概念来设计活动。

3.4.6　思辨听力活动设计六：识别和评价"假设"

1）要点讲解

假设，是我们接受为真或者接受为确实发生过的、不加质疑的事情。简言之，就是信以为真的东西。所有的推理都要有一个起点，假设就是这个起点。值得注意的是，如果假设错了，那么整个推理过程都可能出错。

借一个脑筋急转弯游戏来举例说明。什么时候 1 加 2 不等于 3？其中一个睿智的回答就是：当 1 加 1 不等于 2 的时候。1 加 1 等于 2，是我们信以为真，不加质疑的。这是十进制的规则。如果我们以此为前提来做数学计算，那么 1 加 2 就等于 3。但是，如果 1 加 1 不等于 2（如在二进制里，算法变了），那么 1 加 2 也就不等于 3 了。这个回答的聪明之处就在于找到问题的假设，然后改变它。假设是我们觉得理所当然的东西。因为习以为常，所以我们往往不假思索，不但不清楚自己的假设是什么，而且还发现不了其中可能存在的片面性甚至错误。

日常生活中不乏假设出错的例子。为什么包装靓丽的商品比包装普通的产品有更好的销售量？这就是因为人们不自觉地假设，外包装高档的商品一定也是高质量的。而事实上不少商人正是利用人们的这个思维误区，通过改进包装来提高价格，而不是提升产品质量。在人与人交流时，我们也常常会假设对方与我们的出发点是一样的，而有时候并非如此。结果当双方不能达成一致而发生争执的时候，往往还不清楚是因为什么。

假设是思维的起点。因为很多假设是隐含的，所以识别假设并理性地评价假设，对批评性思维有着非常重要的意义。

2）课前准备

从日常会话到学术讲座，在各种听力材料中都可以找到假设。对话常常可以用来作为练习，特别是当双方表达不同看法的时候，可以窥见不同假设的存在。教师可准备以下问题，来提问学生去识别和评价假设：

- What is the speaker taking for granted?
- What assumptions have been made?
- Are these assumptions justifiable?
- Are they consistent?
- What are my assumptions?

3）活动实例

听前

在思维八要素中，"假设"是一个难点。为让学生更好地识别听力材料中的假设，教师可以在听前用讲故事、话题讨论、师生对话等形式，配合以视频、音频、图片等多媒体输入，设置情境，先让学生了解"假设"是什么。例如，向学生展示农夫山泉的广告图画，即青山绿水和矿泉水瓶，以及"我们不生产水，我们只是大自然的搬运工"这句广告词。这句耳熟能详的广告词隐含什么假设？是否有道理？

听中

本例选取了一篇日常生活中的对话。对话在两位女性之间展开，Akane 询问 Ruth 对做全职母亲这个事情怎么看，Ruth 表达的看法和 Akane 不同。两人讨论的焦点是在全职母亲照顾下长大的孩子是否有更好的社会性。教师让学生们听一遍对话，回答下列问题：

(1) Why does Ruth think it is really bad if a child stays at home with one parent?

(2) Does Akane agree with her? What is Akane's opinion?

(3) What are the assumptions they made about raising children by a stay-at-home parent? Do they have the same assumption?

(4) How do you evaluate their assumptions?

这一练习不采用讨论的方式，而是由学生独立思考后回答，以便从学生的回答看出他们对"假设"这个要素理解得是否准确。

前两题是先让学生明确两人的立场和观点，第三题引导学生思考说话人的假设。通过对两人假设的分析，可以清楚地看出她们产生意见分歧的原因。第四题是要求学生对两人的假设做出评价。实际上，两人都认可培养孩子的社会性是必要的，但是两人对全职母亲有不同的假设。一个人认为全职母亲就是天天自己带孩子，导致孩子接触不到太多其他的人，言下之意是还不如交给托儿所。另一个认为，全职母亲才有更多时间带孩子出去和更多的人交流，反而有利于培养社会性。两人的假设都有一定的合理性，但是都只看到一个方面，因此有些片面。从这个例子还可以看出，即使对于同一个概念，不同人的假设也可能不同。

听后

经过上述练习，学生已经对"假设"这个概念基本掌握，但是仍需巩固。这里补充一些常见的错误假设，让学生识别并说明为什么不合理。

(1) The faster you walk, the closer you get.

(2) Everything happens for a reason.

(3) Someone else will be responsible for this.

(4) You need to be perfect.

(5) All you need is good luck.

(6) Things will work out eventually.

4）音视频文本

Akane: Ruth, what do you think about stay-at-home parents?

Ruth: Do you mean like one parent staying at home with a child?

Akane: Yeah, one parent staying at home and the other one working.

Ruth: Ah, I think it's really bad if a child stays at home with one parent actually.

Akane: Really, why would you say that?

Ruth: I think children who are brought up like that generally don't really know how to socialize with other people except for their parents.

Akane: Oh, well, why would you think that?

Ruth: Well, they're not really given the opportunity to interact with different people, I mean, they spend pretty much all day, every day, with that one parent, and I think it's a real shame. They don't learn how to share or, you know, how to get along with and talk to different people.

Akane: Well, I think that the child will actually get more interaction if there's a stay-at-home parent because the parent will be able to take them to different activities and to other houses to have playmates and at the same time, they'll be able to spend more time with that parent and have socializing time with family members.

Ruth: But I think children could get those same experiences from different people who look after them. It wouldn't necessarily need to be their family who looked after them surely.

Akane: Well, sure but, I think that it's different when a person who is not related takes care of a child. I'm sure that they do their best but the love is not there. The caretaker would not love the child as much as the parent would and at the same time if there's one person taking care of 10 different children at the same time, I would wonder about the amount of attention that the child gets, and safety issues as well.

Ruth: But I think you've got to look at the practical aspect of this. It's not always practical for people who don't have much money to have one parent staying at home all of the time.

Akane: That's true. I really agree about that.

Ruth: Oh, good we agree on one thing.

5）变化与拓展

除了识别别人的假设，反思自己的假设也非常重要。一个善于批判性思维的人会对自己的假设有清楚的认知。另一种听前活动可设计为让学生反思自己是否有如下类似观点：

- I know what I am thinking.
- I am a reasonable person. If you disagree with me, something is wrong with you.
- Everyone else is smarter than me.
- I have enough time to finish the project. I will start tomorrow.

然后组成小组讨论。教师进而讲解假设的定义、如何识别，等等。课堂上还可以就一些普遍性的问题询问学生的假设。他们也许会惊讶地发现不同人的出发点会非常不同。

如果听力材料是对话，还可以将听中活动设计为同桌二人各自扮演对话中的一个角色。将自己摆在说话人的位置上，可以更好地理解说话人的假设并加以判断。

3.4.7　思辨听力活动设计七：识别和评价"蕴意"

1）要点讲解

Paul & Elder（2006）认为，所有的推理都有所指向，可能是隐含的影响、启示或意义，也可能是真实发生的结果，英文是 implications 和 consequences。对这一要素，本书译为蕴意。它表现的是观点或事件之间的逻辑关系。只要我们去思维、去逻辑推理，就自然会有后续。在思辨听力中，我们需要识别的是说话人的推理意味着什么、可能的后果是什么。就如活动四中的例子，说话人提到人们对互联网的社会作用了解甚少，这里隐含着希望人们在这方面加强研究。这篇听力材料的结尾也印证了这一点：互联网创始人创立基金会，让接入互联网成为人的基本权利和全球范围内的公共福利。

在学术领域，我们常常会谈论一个研究的意义（Implications），也就是谈论这个研究的发现对未来意味着什么。例如，我们发现学生的动机越高，他们的语言技能就学得越好。这一发现就意味着通过改变动机能够影响语言技能的学习，教师应当重视激发学生的学习动机。Consequence 通常指不愉快的或者不希望看到的结果，也是依据逻辑推理所得出的，如全球变暖的后果。

2）课前准备

听新闻报道可以用来练习对蕴意的识别和评价。选择一篇新闻报道，分析其中的事件及其蕴意、影响或后果，准备以下的问题：

- What does the statement imply?
- What are the implications of the speaker's reasoning?
- How significant are the implications?
- What other implications and/or possible consequences might follow?

3）活动实例

听前

这一篇新闻报道讲的是美国大学学费上涨的原因和后果。听者必须梳理出里面的逻辑关系，才能对这篇报道做批判性的分析。听前，教师布置学生围绕这一话题展开小组讨论，任务是列出导致学费上涨的可能因素，讨论中允许学生查阅互联网资料。

听中

这篇材料语速稍快，学生听 2—3 遍后，回答下列问题：

1) According to the sources in the news, why do universities charge higher tuition fees than before? What is the implication?

2) Experts worry that the high cost of college makes it less likely for bright students from poor families to attend college. What does this claim imply? Any consequences?

3）Georgetown University Labor Economist Anthony Carnevale says the current system is unsustainable for families and cuts economic growth for the whole country. What does he imply?

大学校方认为，招生人数虽然增加了，但是政府给大学的财政支出却减少了。为了付给教授们体面的工资以留住他们，校方只有提高学费。这一做法可能带来的后果是，那些非常优秀的、本可以成为科学家、工程师、医生或者教师的中学生，却被高昂的学费挡在了大学校门外。其他的后果还包括国家经济的下滑，因为更多的毕业生不得不贷款上大学，他们在大学毕业后必须偿还贷款，因而推迟结婚、生子和大宗购买。劳工经济学家 Anthony Carnevale 认为目前提高学费的做法是不可持续的，势必会影响经济发展。他的观点有一个隐含的意思，就是如果大学和政府不改进现在的制度，那么国家的生产力就会下降。审视整篇材料从原因到后果的推理，我们认为这样的担心是有道理的。

听后

教师将本篇听力材料的文本显示在屏幕上，和同学们一起讨论它的结构。首先，材料中讲述了一件真人真事：Joshua Jordan 的学位很光鲜，但是学生贷款压得他喘不过气；接下来讲述普遍情况，引入专家评论，分析原因和后果；最后是结尾部分，还是引用了 Joshua Jordan 的话，呼应开头。教师提醒学生，在新闻报道的结构中 implications 和 consequences 的出现位置通常在中间靠后，在以后的听力活动中还需注意归纳。

4）音视频文本

Joshua Jordan earned a doctorate degree in physical therapy. He hopes to open his own practice someday, and says having the expensive graduate degree is good for his patients, but hard on his wallet.

"I am currently in debt for $210,000," he said.

Jordan's loans are eight times larger than those of the average student. He says it might take him 20 years to pay them off, and he has sometimes had to work two jobs at a time to meet his bills.

For the past 30 years, college tuition has been going up at twice the rate of inflation, and private colleges now charge an average of more than $30,000 a year.

Universities say they're caught between record-high enrollments, a workforce of professors who have the skills to find work elsewhere if they are not well paid, and falling financial support from state governments.

Terry Hartle speaks for the American Council on Education which represents thousands of colleges and universities across the United States.

"It's a terrible conundrum that we face as a country. We want more and more post-secondary education. We want more focus on academic quality and graduation. At the same point, the funding sources for higher education have been diminishing for a generation."

While these students made it to graduation, experts worry the high cost of college makes it less likely that bright students from poor families will attend college, depriving the economy of some of the scientists, engineers and others who could help boost growth.

And a survey shows that some students concerned about repaying thousands of dollars in loans are putting off marriage, children, and the major purchases that usually go along with forming a family.

Peter Mazareas is with the College Savings Foundation. "These students just will not contribute to the economy. They'll go home and live at home. They won't buy cars. They won't invest in housing, so there is a real multiplier effect that is short term."

Georgetown University Labor Economist Anthony Carnevale says the current system is unsustainable for families and cuts economic growth for the whole country. "The effects on economic growth are substantial. If we had kept up with the demand for post-secondary talent, economists estimate that we would be at about $500 billion more per annum in gross domestic product, i.e., people would have more money to spend. There would have been a higher productivity rate."

Meanwhile, Jordan says his family is not wealthy and could not have paid for so many years in so many colleges on the way to a PhD.

"There would have been no way I could have created a career for myself that I wanted to do without the use of student loans."

So, for him, it's worth it.

5）变化与拓展

蕴意是因推理而产生的，我们应注意把控自己推理的方向，尽量准确地识别所听材料中的蕴意和后果。另外，学到此处，还要注意把本课所学的思维要素（蕴意）与之前所学的思维要素（如推断、假设）加以区别。可设计的拓展活动是基于一个听力材料，就两个或多个思辨要素的识别和评价进行提问。

3.4.8　思辨听力活动设计八：识别和评价"观点"

1）要点讲解

观点与视角有关。视角，就是看问题的角度。看问题的角度不同，很可能导致观点不同。这里，我们不仅要注意看问题的出发点，还要注意看的对象以及看的方式。人类的思维具有相对性和选择性，我们并不能同时看到一个人或者一件事的各个方面。盲人摸象的寓意就是如此。摸象的人只接触到局部，却以为自己看到了全貌。

这个寓言中的盲人，其实就是我们自身的写照。我们总以为自己掌握了绝对的真理，而看不到自身的见识可能有限、自我的经验可能主观、别人正确的观点可能被自己忽略。事实上，个人的观点常常只反映了问题的一个方面。作为思辨技能的学习者，我们应该知道放开眼界，意识到不同视角的存在，学会了解他人的观点以超越自己的局限，并且在评价他人的观点时力求公正。在处理那些本来就有争议的论题上，这一点尤其重要。

2）课前准备

可选择内容中含有不同视角的听力材料，或者较之平常视角有独特之处的材料。可准备以下的问题：

- What are the main points of view in the listening material?
- Does the speaker consider other relevant points of view?
- Should we consider multiple points of view to reason well through the issue?
- Given the situation, which of these perspectives seems more reasonable?
- What are the most important aspects of the problem from the point of view of relevant others?

3）活动实例

听前

本例谈论的主题是社交媒体。社交媒体对人类的影响是颇具争议的话题。从科技的角度来看，社交媒体以及互联网和智能手机，都极大地改变了人们的社交方式，使人可以在任何时候、任何地点展开交流。然而，社交媒体也存在问题。听前，教师请学生在小组中展开"模拟采访"的活动，任务是列出社交媒体的优缺点。学生组成 4—5 人的小组，轮流担任采访者、被访者和记录员。被访者还可以为自己设计不同的身份。

听中

听 1—2 遍，回答如下的问题：

1) What effects does social media have on human communication from a technological point of view?

2) What effects does social media have on human beings from a psychological point of view?

3) What does the speaker think of social media? What is his point of view?

4) What do you think of his ideas?

社交媒体的缺点是它会使人上瘾，晒图等行为还加剧了人们之间的攀比，引发嫉妒心。所以，从心理学上说，社交媒体是有弊端的。那么，从脑科学的角度看，社交媒体是怎样的？这篇听力材料给出了脑科学家的观点。这一部分有些专业术语，可多听一遍。

听后

教师先总结文中的观点，再加上听前练习中学生们的观点，重申看一个问题可以有不同的角度，不同观点之间的关系也是复杂的，有的对立，有的互补。思考问题要全面，就是指要从多个角度看问题。教师还可指出，导致视角狭隘而不能全面公正看待问题的原因，有时是视角的局限，有时是参照系的缺失。思辨者应努力做到全面谨慎地思考问题，重视思辨的每一个要素。

4）音视频文本

Social media is a fascinating new human phenomenon. And when we look at it deeply from a brain point of view, when we start with the foundation that the brain is actually the social organ of the body, we can understand why social media and brain functions would go hand in hand. That is, the reason social media took off in the last ten years is that the brain is social and people really want to connect with each other. And then when social media was designed and keeps on creating itself, then the social media in fact is going to be shaping the brain so that the brain is responsive to culture. And in one of our research centers at UCLA, what we're able to show is that cultural experiences, that is, messages sent out in society, better mediated through communication, one on one or mass media communication, actually shape the actual structure of the brain. And so it's a two-way street. The brain created social media. And social media shapes the brain.

One of the simple things I think that social media does is it brings us back at least to a feeling on one level, that we're having the connections that we evolve to have. It's a great question, you know: Is social media replacing our relationships? Or is it adding to it? From a brain point of view, the difference between, let's say, e-mail and social media versus face-to-face interactions is very interesting. So, there are studies, for example, that have shown what it's like when you actually are with someone face-to-face where you have eye contact, that you're sharing facial expressions. And there's a tone of voice you can hear, the posture of the person, the gestures, the timing of what they do, the intensity of what they respond with. Those seven signals. And those are eye contact, facial expression, tone of voice, posture, gestures, timing, intensity. If you memorize those, it's really useful because then you'll see what texting, what e-mail and what most social media actually is lacking. Now when you look at what area of the brain both sends out those nonverbal signals and receives them and makes sense of them, it's the right hemisphere of the brain. And the right hemisphere of the brain is much more closely connected to the lower regions. So, the higher right areas are connected to the lower regions of the brain and those lower regions work with the body itself to create our emotions, to give us the felt texture of lived life. So, one deep concern that I have, as a developmental theorist and developmental clinician, is that the more people spend time not using nonverbal signals and instead use mostly verbal ones, that is, text with language that has this linear way of being distributed, the more you are activating primarily your left hemisphere which in the brain is much more distant from the lower areas that help mediate emotion with the body. And even autobiographical memory is dominant on the right side. So, you're much more into just logistics. Even thinking about how people are gonna care about you or like you is a left brain thing. Just fascinating. It's called social display rules. So, from a hemisphere point of view, what I'm deeply concerned about is if social media, e-mail, texting are not actually getting people more face-to-face time with each other or getting them in touch with even what's going on inside of them, then the new generation will be much more used to a very surface level of experiencing the world.

So, there's nothing inherently wrong with social media. But if it is replacing time for face-to-face, then that could be a big problem.

5）变化与拓展

听前活动的另外一个形式是，教师播放听力材料的开头部分，暂停，让学生陈述各自的预测，起到 warming up 的作用，然后听完整的篇章。如果材料的主旨与预测并不一致，往往会给学生留下更为深刻的印象。接下来，教师提出上述问题，学生完整地听第二遍，再对问题作答。

第四章　跨文化听力活动

4.1　跨文化听力的情境案例

　　一位去英国留学的学生跟我分享了一些有趣的经历。刚到英国不久，她就发现自己在理解英国人说话时有些偏差。英国人看似表达积极意思的用词，却未必表达积极的意思。英国人语气平淡地说 quite good 时，实际上可能是在说"还行（甚至不太好）"；英国同学评价她的课堂发言时说"I think the presentation is quite good, but…"，紧接着提出好几个建议，可见"quite good"只是客套话，好像只有说"excellent"或"fantastic"且没什么意见时，才表明是真的好；老师上课点评说的"That's a very interesting point."也不一定是说你的观点多么有趣，甚至可能表示你有点跑题了。

　　她发现英国人说话比较委婉，不论是教授还是出租车司机皆然，如常常用虚拟语气以示礼貌。她照字面意思理解，就误解过别人的意图。例如，在小组讨论时，一位同学说完观点，其他同学在回应时通常会说"I would suggest…""Perhaps we could consider…""Why don't we…"，等等。她开始以为这些是在表达"我有个建议，大家一起商量商量"等意思，后来才发现这些其实是在表达反对意见。"I'm not sure about that.""I see it differently.""I can see your point, but…"都是用来引出不同的观点。"I just think it would be really nice if we…"不是"做了会很好、不做没关系"，而是明确表达希望去做；"Correct me if I'm wrong, but I think…"也并非真的让你纠正他们，只是习惯性的委婉表达而已。

　　这位学生还举了两个例子。听到宿舍管理员催缴住宿费时说"Could you please…""I would appreciate it if you…"，她还以为对方没那么着急；另有一次，她和英国同学在餐厅讨论作业，工作人员走过来说这里要接待重要来宾，学生不可以坐。几经交涉后对方说："You can't stay here. Please leave."看到英国同学听到这句话非常生气时，她觉得有些小题大做，后来才明白这种命令句语气，即使有一个"please"在里面，也已经相当不礼貌了。

　　这些看似微小的语言交际问题，反映了怎样的文化现象？怎样才能"听懂"它们？

20 年前，世界各国在面临世纪更迭之际，都将教育视作开启未来的钥匙。未来的世界是怎样的？应该培养什么样的人才来迎接未来？全球化的事实，使越来越多的教育者相信，高等教育应该承担培养跨文化人才的任务，跨文化能力和多样性应该摆上教育的议事日程（Deardorff 2011）。当年，在"如何为下一个世纪准备人才"的思考中，世界各国不约而同地将交际能力作为未来的重要能力来培养。美国和欧盟将语言教学的重点从听说读写的技能训练转向交际能力培养，强调个体的参与和在社会中与他人的相互交流。相关内容可参见《外语学习标准：为 21 世纪做准备》（*Standards for Foreign Language Learning: Preparing for the 21st Century*）（ACTFL，1996）和《欧洲语言共同参考框架：学习、教学、评估》（欧洲理事会文化合作教育委员会，2008）。

2018 年，我国颁布的《国标》将跨文化交流能力列为外语类专业学生的能力要求。"跨文化交际"成为专业核心课程。根据《国标》要求，外语类专业必须把跨文化教育贯穿到整个课程体系和每个教学环节。可见，在中外文明互鉴的时代大背景下，加强培养具有跨文化能力的国际化外语人才，是我国全方位走向世界的人才急需，也是新时期的中国高等教育应尽快肩负起的紧迫使命（孙有中 2016）。

　　改革开放以来，我国的外语教育获得了极大的发展。但是，由于客观条件限制，交际能力的发展还存在很大空间。学生学习外语主要依赖于课堂和课本，在真实语境中的交际能力锻炼比较少，因此不能将外语能力简单等同于交际能力。我国学者文秋芳（1999）认为，在外语教学中不能将外语水平等同于交际能力，由于跨文化交际中存在文化差异，因此外语教学中的重点是要使学生具有处理文化差异的能力，应培养学生的语言能力、语用能力和策略能力，对文化差异的敏感性、宽容性以及处理文化差异的灵活性（转引自葛春萍、王守仁 2016）。文秋芳（2016：1）还认为，在英语作为通用语的背景下，应重新认识语言与文化的关系，鼓励学习者学习多元文化，包括目标语文化、本土文化和其他国家文化，培养他们既要熟悉交际对方的文化传统和思维方式，也要具备在跨文化交流中所应有的民族文化自信和自觉，实现中国文化走出去的目标。

那么，什么是跨文化听力？怎样在听力课堂上提高跨文化能力？教师该怎样设计课堂活动？本章旨在为这些问题找到答案。

4.2 跨文化听力的理论框架

4.2.1 跨文化能力

在定义跨文化听力之前，我们需要先回顾跨文化能力的内涵。有关跨文化能力（Intercultural Competence）这一概念的术语尚不统一。对此，不同的研究领域有不同的名称，如 cultural competence 或 global competence、multicultural competence、intercultural communication competence，甚至还有 cultural intelligence、cross-cultural awareness、intercultural maturity，等等（Deardorff 2011；Fantini 2009）。

那么，跨文化交际能力和跨文化能力又有什么不同？高永晨（2014）用"等同说""大于说"和"小于说"进行了分类。持"等同说"的人认为两者没有区别，可以通用（如 Chen 2010；Lustig & Koester 2006；庄恩平 2006）。但是，"大于说"认为跨文化交际能力除了跨文化能力，还需要具备语言能力、社会语言能力和语篇能力（Byram 1997）。文秋芳（1999）也持类似观点，认为跨文化交际能力由交际能力和跨文化能力组成。"小于说"则认为跨文化能力是一个较大的概念，跨文化交际能力是其中一个方面。

笔者认为，虽然听力课堂上注重的是跨文化交际能力的培养，但其内涵与跨文化能力是共通的。听力课堂本身就是一个锻炼语言能力的环境。因为无论从上面哪种角度来说，将跨文化能力等同于跨文化交际能力，都没有太大问题。学界也有此先例（如胡文仲 2013）。本书亦将此两种提法视为同一种能力，并使用"跨文化能力"这一表述。

根据学界普遍接受的定义，跨文化能力是指能与来自不同文化背景的人有效而恰当地交往的能力。西方的跨文化研究已经有超过 50 年的历史，留下了无数的定义和框架，直到 Deardorff（2006）使用"德尔斐方法"（the Delphi technique，一种在专家之间不断迭代而达成共识的方法），才就跨文化能力的定义达成共识。之后，Deardorff（2006）根据共识进一步分类，并在理论框架中引入更为具体的内涵，即认为跨文化能力是指发展跨文化交际所需的知识、技能和态度的能力，并指出正是这种能力使人能够在跨文化互动中产生有效和恰当的交际行为。McKinnon（2013）将 Deardorff（2006）的理论用图简洁表述如下（如图 4.1）并进行了解读。

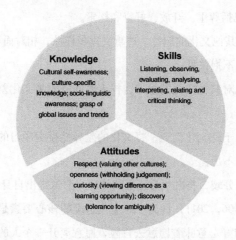

图 4.1：跨文化能力内涵（Deardorff 2006；改编自 McKinnon 2013）

跨文化知识

跨文化知识包括文化自我意识、文化专门知识、社会语言学意识和对全球事件和趋势的把握。

- 文化自我意识：能清楚地表达自己的文化如何塑造了自己的身份和世界观；
- 文化专门知识：能分析和解释其他文化的基本信息（历史、价值观、政治、经济、交际风格、信仰与实践）；
- 社会语言学意识：能获取当地的语言知识，能用语言或非语言交流方式表达语言的不同，能调整自己的表达方式来适应其他文化的国民；

- 对全球事件和趋势的把握：能解释全球化的概念和涵义，并能将本土事件与全球大势关联起来。

跨文化技能

跨文化技能包括聆听、观察、评价、分析、阐释、关联和思辨。

- 聆听、观察、评价：通过自己的耐心和坚持去识别并减弱民族中心主义，寻找文化线索和文化含义；
- 分析、阐释、关联：采用对比分析的方法，发现联系、因果和关系；
- 思辨：从其他文化的角度来看待和解释这个世界，并识别自己的视角。

跨文化态度

跨文化态度包括尊重、开放、好奇和探索。

- 尊重：寻找其他文化的属性，尊重文化多样性，相对而不是绝对地思考，对文化差异不抱偏见；
- 开放：搁置对其他文化的批评、投入时间去收集文化差异的证据、愿意被别人挑错；
- 好奇：致力于跨文化沟通，将文化的差异性视为学习的机会，能意识到自己知识的不足；
- 探索：容忍分歧，将之视为正面的体验；愿意走出自身的舒适区。

Deardorff（2006，2011）认为，跨文化态度的核心要素是尊重、开放、好奇和探索。开放和好奇意味着愿意去冒险，愿意离开一个人的舒适区去发现新的事物；而在交际中尊重对方，就是向对方表示自己看重对方的文化。这一点是平等交往的前提。这些态度，对进一步发展跨文化交际所需的知识和技能来说，是重要的基础。

Martin & Nakayama（2004）和 Odgers（2009）提出好奇、冒险导向、容忍分歧、有同理心、开放、自我反思、尊重差别、幽默等八条跨文化态度。具体包括：要对其他文化抱有好奇心；敢于在不熟悉的环境下交流；勇于犯错并从错误中学习；容忍不同看法和做法；能将自己设于别人的境地来思考问题；能保持开放的心态、不妄加评判；能反思自己的态度和行为；对文化差别予以尊重；能以幽默来化解跨文化交际中的尴尬；等等。

以上介绍了国内外学者对跨文化能力内涵的论述。那么，如果从教学实际出发，我们应该做到什么？《国标》(2018) 对跨文化能力给出的定义如下：

- 尊重世界文化多样性，具有跨文化同理心和批判性文化意识；
- 掌握基本的跨文化研究理论知识和分析方法，理解中外文化的基本特点和异同；
- 能对不同文化现象、文本和制品进行阐释和评价；
- 能有效和恰当地进行跨文化沟通；
- 能帮助不同文化背景的人士进行有效的跨文化沟通。

根据《国标》所给出的定义，结合国内外学者对跨文化能力内涵的讨论，我们能够更加深入地了解跨文化听力的概念。

4.2.2　跨文化听力

我们已经看到，在上文所述的跨文化技能列表中，"听"被排在第一位。实际上，听在跨文化交际中具有极为重要的地位。倾听是人与人之间相互理解的最佳方式 (Clinard 1985)。倾听有助于交流双方建立良好而深厚的关系。有效的倾听能使交流富有成效。

怎样才能做到有效地倾听？中华文化对此有着自己独到的见解。Beall (2010) 发现，中文"听"字的繁体形式，用奇妙的方式传达了中华文化对"听"的理解，同时也阐述了"听"与跨文化交流的关系（见图 4.2）。从偏旁部首可以看出，"听"不但要用耳聆听，还要用眼观察、用心去思考，要一心一意，也就是要用全身心去理解。中文"听"的繁体形式完美地体现了我们在跨文化交流中应秉持的态度，即我们既要敏锐地用耳、用眼、用心去感知文化差异，也要通过思考，去审慎判断并吸收多元文化的精华，具备同理心（王艳 2018）。从这里也可以看出，学会倾听，不但可以锻炼跨文化交流技能，还有助于培养正确的跨文化交流态度。

图 4.2　繁体"听"字对跨文化概念的启示

听能够促进跨文化能力，反过来，文化因素对"听"有着不可忽视的影响。Wolvin & Coakley（1996）认为，在所有交流行为（包括听）当中，文化因素是最首要的决定因素。正如交流与文化密不可分一样，"听"与文化也密不可分。Faerch & Kasper（1986）将社会文化能力（即对说话者话语中传递的社会文化信息的熟悉程度）列入对听力理解的影响因素。可见，培养跨文化倾听的能力既能够提高跨文化能力，又能促进听力理解，理应成为听力教学的重要目标和内容。

传统的听力课，不能说没有与跨文化交际相关的内容。但是，仅仅涉及文化话题，与系统地发展跨文化能力相比，还是有很大的区别。跨文化交际的专门课程是必要的，但是跨文化能力也要融入到具体课程中去培养。跨文化听力就是这样的一种实践。这种听力活动的目标就是本着尊重、开放、好奇和探索的态度，运用自己对双方的文化知识、社会语言学知识和对当今世界的了解，去聆听、观察、分析、阐释和评价视听材料中的文化信息，解决其中所呈现的跨文化问题。

跨文化能力的培养是一个长期的过程，除了课堂上的系统学习，课外还应尽量增加跨文化交流的机会。与来自目的语国家的学生交流或前往目的语国家学习生活都是非常好的提高跨文化能力的机会。但是国情所限，大部分中国学习者依赖的仍然是课堂。外语视听课应积极创造学习机会，将交际场景呈现在课堂设计的活动中，通过教师讲解和同伴互动，为学生将来在真实的跨文化情境下进行有效而恰当的交流，打下良好的基础。

4.3　跨文化听力的教学目标

孙有中（2016）提出跨文化教学五原则，简称为 CREED，即思辨（Critiquing）、反省（Reflecting）、探究（Exploring）、共情（Empathizing）和体验（Doing），为培养跨文化倾听的能力提供了解决方案。根据这一原则，跨文化听力教学可以运用思辨的方法对跨文化知识、信息和案例进行分析和评价；将跨文化知识和理论运用于自己对视听材料的理解，运用于中外文化之间的对比与反思，增强文化自信；以探究式学习方式获取信息，寻求资源，独立思考，解决跨文化问题；包容文化差异，乐于换位思考，在比较文化差异的基础上理解和感受差异，做出审慎的评价；在体验中学习，既可以通过聆听跨文化案例、观赏跨文化电影、扮演跨文化角色等活动间接地体验跨文化沟通，也可以通过国际交流学习来直接体验。这些原则可用来指导教学目标的设立。

在以培养跨文化能力为目标的听力课堂上，我们主要关注的是所听材料中的文化现象。教学目标可设定为识别、阐释、对比和评价听力材料中的文化现象。

4.3.1　识别听力材料中的文化现象

与来自不同文化的人进行交流，也许会遇到秉持相近的信仰、观点和思维方式的人，也有可能会遇到在这些方面与自己完全不同的人。这时，要能够敏锐地感知相似和不同，则必须具备对自我文化的清楚认识和对他人文化的充分了解。因此，学习者应首先学会去发现透露文化信息的线索，识别所听材料中的文化现象。这些线索包括音视频材料中所含有的语言信息和非语言信息（如身势语等）。

4.3.2　阐释听力材料中的文化现象

在跨文化交流中，学习者应能用流畅的语言阐释文化现象，即准确描述和说明这一现象并解释其背后的文化。这是对跨文化知识的显性运用。平时，学习者可以通过跨文化课程进行系统的学习，或通过听新闻、看小说、欣赏影视剧等进行碎片化的积累。这一教学目标使学习者能够运用和验证自己已有的中外文化知识，同时也能学习到新的跨文化知识。学习者尤其应能阐释自己的文化，如中国学生应能够用英文熟练表达中华文化的价值观。

4.3.3 对比听力材料中的文化现象

学习者应能够对听力材料中不同的文化现象进行对比，包括中外对比和不同外国文化之间的对比。通过对比，能促使学习者去寻找重要细节，归纳特征，发现区别与联系，从而达到对文化现象的深入理解。对比还有助于发现新旧事物的关联，有利于学习者跨文化知识的增长。对比听力材料中的文化现象，为下一步跨文化评价打下基础。

4.3.4 评价听力材料中的文化现象

学习者应能够对文化现象进行评价，达到理解多元文化异同、提高文明互鉴意识的目的。这一目标是这四个教学目标中最具难度的。评价既涉及标准，也涉及态度，其本身就是思辨的一个重要环节，是高阶思维的组成部分，也是跨文化能力的综合体现。对所听材料从识别到阐述，再到对比和评价，是逐步提升跨文化能力的阶梯。

4.4 跨文化听力教学设计实例

这一部分将针对教学目标设计教学活动。以下每个教学活动包括知识要点的讲解、课前准备、活动实例、音视频材料的文本和变化与拓展等五个方面。

4.4.1 跨文化听力活动设计一：文化自我意识的表达

1）要点讲解

文化自我意识是跨文化知识学习的首要内容。学生应清楚了解自己国家的文化是怎样塑造自己的身份和价值观的。在本活动中，学生先倾听别人描述自己的文化，再学会将自己本民族的文化特点用英文恰当地表达出来。这一视听说活动的目的，首先是帮助学生在了解世界各地不同文化的同时，认识本国文化的独特性；其次是通过对听力材料中文化现象的识别和对比，学会阐释本民族文化的特点，提升文化自信；最后是培养跨文化交流中相互尊重的态度和开放的心态。

2）课前准备

（1）设计任务场景，如在与国际学生的交谈中描述自己的文化、在国外的跨文化课程上介绍自己国家的文化，等等。

（2）根据听力材料，准备启发学生深入理解和引导学生完成任务的问题。

（3）介绍中国文化的英文资源很多，包括文章、图片、音视频等，从中挑选一些制作成幻灯片。也可以准备世界地图和相关国家地图备用。

3）活动实例

听前

本听力材料选自一档文化专题节目，参与者分别来自亚洲、南美洲、欧洲和非洲的不同国家和地区（巴基斯坦、印度、日本、牙买加、纳米比亚以及中东地区，等等），他们从不同侧面描述了自己的文化。听前，教师可请几位学生分别简要讲述自己对其中一个国家的了解。

听中

听1—2遍，然后让学生准备一个介绍中国文化的三分钟发言。教师可准备以下问题来引导学生完成任务：

- What does Mahmood Jamal mean by saying he did not know who he was when he first came to the UK?

- How did Eilidh Hamilton describe the culture in the Middle East?

- What adjectives did Rajni Baldani use to describe the Indian culture?

- What can we infer from what Kyung-Ja Yoo said about her culture?

- Do Jamaica and Namibia share anything in common in culture?

当一个人身处别的文化中时，反而能更敏锐地觉察自己的身份。也就是说，通过发现别人更好地发现了自己。这也是第一题中 Mahmood Jamal 所表达的意思。Eilidh Hamilton 说到自己文化中的宿命观；Rajni Baldani 用 vibrant、diverse、complex 和 rich 来形容印度的文化；从 Kyung-Ja Yoo 举的例子当中，我们推断出日本文化中男女地位的不同；牙买加和纳米比亚的文化气质，一个热情奔放，一个安静平和。至少从这篇材料的描述来看，各国文化是相当不同的。听到他们谈论自己的文化，我们的文化自我意识是否更为清晰了呢？哪些形容词可用来描述中国文化？哪些例子可用来阐释中国文化？怎样通过与别的文化对比来讲述中国文化的特点？

听后

在几分钟内完整描述自己国家或民族的文化是很难的，学生们一般会从某些具体层面谈起，如历史、饮食、家庭观念，等等。除了这些，中国文化还有哪些总体特征？你的介绍是否涵盖了中国文化的某个核心特征？是否有自己的切身感受？条理是否清楚？在听后活动中，教师还可用这些问题引导学生深入思考并完善文化自我意识的表达。

4）音视频文本

Mahmood Jamal（巴基斯坦）

When I first came to Britain I did not know who I was. Over the years I began to discover, as I discovered Britain, I also discovered myself. And this is also very important in people who move from one culture to another, one place to another because it's not just discovering the other places, you also discover who you are.

Eilidh Hamilton（中东地区）

En-shala is a very popular phrase in the Middle East. It means "if it is the will of God" literally. Now it doesn't necessarily have such overt religious connotations as we might expect. But what it does reflect is a certain fatalism amongst many people. They feel that life is, to an extent, controlled by external factors. So the concept of the Westerner as someone who is constantly striving to improve themselves and their situation is anathema to people there who don't feel that there's very much in a practical way they can do to change that.

Rajni Baldani（印度）

I would describe my culture, the Indian culture, as being extremely vibrant, and diverse, complex, in every aspect – art, literature, folk, the oral tradition. We are really very rich in all aspects.

Dionne Charmaine（牙买加）

Silence in Jamaica is a good thing. It's very much a sign of respect and if you're basically being spoken to – especially by someone that's older than you and so on, and you raise your voice, then that's being disrespectful. Jamaicans as a people we're very, very, very proud people and they have a lot to say about a lot of things. When we believe in something, we tend to put that across very passionately and it can come over as being too direct or aggressive, or too insensitive sometimes. But it is, you know, as you get to know the people, you'll find that it's just that they're so passionate.

Kyung-Ja Yoo（日本）

In Japan, what's supposed to happen is a woman should follow a man and then you are supposed to walk behind him, three steps behind.

Emma Kambangula（纳米比亚）

I think Namibia is more of a silent culture. But I prefer our way of communicating to being loud and letting everyone know, because we believe in Namibia not to hang your dirty laundry in public. We are kind of quiet people, not aggressive. We don't like violence. And that's one thing I love among my people.

（说明：括号内为说话人来自的国家或地区）

5）变化与拓展

这个活动还可以变换一种方式：在听之前，教师请学生们组成 3—4 人小组，用 5—10 分钟的时间讨论应如何描述自己国家的文化，然后请一位学生代表小组发言，全班同学聆听并归纳、总结文化描述的内容和方式。然后播放音频材料 1—2 遍，听完后教师提问前述 5 个问题，以加深学生对文化描述内容和方法的理解。随后，学生们再次回到小组，共同完成对本国文化的描述。

4.4.2 跨文化听力活动设计二：其他文化基本信息的识别

1）要点讲解

时间观是重要的文化基本信息。时间观，或者说时间取向，反映了一个民族或一种文化的价值观念、行为规范、传统习俗和风土人情。不同文化有着不同的时间观。有关不同文化之间的时间意识、时间态度和时间观念等方面的知识折射出文化的深层内涵，是文化专门知识的重要组成部分。

时间意识分为主观时间和客观时间，时间态度分为过去时间取向、现在时间取向和未来时间取向，时间观念分为单向性和多向性时间。不同文化中的人们在工作节奏、竞争意识、是否守时、是否计划未来、是否看重传统等方面存在不同，可以用这些概念加以解释和分类。

值得注意的是，文化会随着时代的变迁而变化，文化之间也存在相互碰撞和交融。在解释和分析跨文化现象时应采用发展变化的视角，避免形成刻板印象，既考虑到普遍性，也看到特殊性。

2）课前准备

（1）设计任务场景，如在不同国家，如果有朋友请你赴宴，你应该几点到场；当你有事想要离开，你应该怎样提出，等等。

（2）准备以不同时间观为主题的视听材料。

（3）准备趣味测试题，将各国人对时间的不同意识和态度做成选项。

(4) 补充必要的阅读材料，或涉及时间观的电影、电视剧片段。

3）活动实例

听前

本听力材料与前一个材料来源相同，选自同一档文化专题节目。这一次，参与者分别谈论了自己国家的时间观。听前，教师利用趣味小测试来激发学生对不同国家文化信息的兴趣，比如采用智力抢答的形式，将各国人时间观的不同表现做成选项，让学生们竞答，作为热身活动。以下为一例：

In (country name), you're expected to arrive _____ for business meetings.

A. on time　　　　　B. early　　　　　C. late

听中

教师将提前准备的问题显示在屏幕上，引导学生识别不同文化的时间观。

- Do Brazilian Indians believe that every minute matters?
- Why does Rajni Badlani say that Indian Standard Time is a joke?
- How does Eilidh Hamilton explain that people in her country are usually not punctual?
- Which culture does James Keegan come from?

有研究认为，有悠久古代文明的国家大都具有过去时间倾向，重视历史和过去，因而做事比较遵守传统。西方人，尤其是英美人，着眼未来，是未来时间取向。还有一些文化着眼现在，比如美洲印第安人认为他们的行为只对现在而言，没有过去和未来，他们的语言中甚至没有时间延迟和等待这样的词汇（关世杰 1995）。阿拉伯文化也属于过去主导型。他们没有一个清晰指向，约定的时间往往比较模糊，约会迟到很常见，等待方也并不懊恼，反而认为这样是为双方留足充裕的准备时间。相比之下，英美文化时间观准确，人们珍惜时间，按时赴约，也有提前预约的习惯。本听力材料中的观点有一定的代表性。

听后

教师需要提醒学生，应注意时代变化对时间观的影响，避免形成刻板印象。互联网的发展就在一定程度上加速了不同文化之间的相互碰撞和相互融合。

4）音视频文本

Ana Baltazar

In the case of the Brazilian Indians, I believe that the question of time and space is completely related. They build their houses in a very particular way, completely related to time, the position of the sun and things like that. This thing of time is not like our time today – like every minute really matters, but for them it's like longer time but they are completely aware of it – and they are kind of really using time but in a more patient way, I believe.

Rajni Badlani

We have this phrase called Indian Standard Time, which is a joke. Which is like always being half an hour late, one hour late. But increasingly now with globalization, and with having to deal with people from outside India, lots of people are becoming aware they need to keep appointments, and see the value of time.

Eilidh Hamilton

I think people do have an image of Arabs as being very late which is not necessarily fair. What people do there is they tend to allow a much greater period of time for each social engagement. So perhaps if you were invited for lunch at two, you would expect to remain with your hosts until the evening. Whereas perhaps in Europe you might go at 2:00 and have left by 4:30. Because of that, perhaps, people aren't necessarily as punctual as we would expect them to be because there's much greater leeway in terms of the time.

James Keegan

We're a society that likes to save time. Time is of essence. There's no doubt about it. From a non-North American perspective, we can seem very abrupt, we can seem too familiar, and we can seem as though we're in a hurry. We're a can-do society. I'm always in awe of the fact that people around me, village people and so on, can actually get things done, get organised, and move ahead very quickly. And then at other times, I'm absolutely frustrated because we've gone ahead and done something that we haven't thought enough about.

5）变化与拓展

在跨文化交际中，敏锐识别其他文化信息是一项重要的技能。在设计识别文化信息的活动时，除了时间观，还有婚姻观、育儿观、教育观等都可以用来作为识别文化信息的参考。外国影片本身就是一个富含文化信息的来源，可挑选使用。

4.4.3　跨文化听力活动设计三：不同文化现象的对比分析

1）要点讲解

对于不同文化现象，我们最常做的就是对比。对比的过程包含不同的步骤。当我们遇到跨文化现象，通常先看到的是表象，需要经过阐释和分析，才能发现现象之间的联系和现象背后的原因，才能对不同文化有更深刻的感悟。在跨文化对比中，应注意引导学生理性把握中外文化的异同，既能保持文化自信，又能意识到某些传统文化的局限性，积极参与新时代中国文化的创新。

2）课前准备

（1）根据听力材料，准备涉及跨文化知识及跨文化分析的相关术语，如 collectivist culture、individualist culture、cultural identity、macroculture、microculture、subculture，等等。此例中需要的是 collectivist culture 和 individualist culture。

（2）设计听前热身活动的任务场景和话题。

（3）准备适合文化对比的影视剧、纪录片。

3）活动实例

听前

本例中的活动要求学生能将自己文化中的教育观念与其他国家的教育观念作对比。中外教育对比是十分常见和热门的话题，既可能发生在日常聊天中，也可以是正式讲座的主题。学生一般都比较熟悉这类话题，但是未必能够有条理地梳理、归纳。因此，教师把听前任务布置为与同桌讨论"可以从哪些维度进行对比"。

听中

这一篇听力材料是比较来自不同文化的学生的课堂行为。教师让学生听1—2遍，听完之后把听力材料中的学生行为从文化层面进行分类，独自完成或小组讨论均可。例如，可从个人主义和集体主义层面来分类：

Individualist Perspective	Collectivist Perspective
• Students work independently; helping others may be cheating. • Students engage in discussion and argument to learn to think critically. • Teacher manages the school environment indirectly and encourages student self-control. • Parents are integral to children's academic progress and participate actively.	• Students work with peers and provide assistance when needed. • Students are quiet and respectful in class in order to learn more efficiently. • Teacher is the primary authority, but peers guide each other's behavior. • Parents yield to teachers' expertise to provide academic instruction and guidance.

听后

文化传统影响一个国家的教育理念，反过来，教育理念也是文化传统的一部分。教师提醒学生不要一边倒地肯定或者否定一种教育模式，而是需要广泛收集资料，充分分析、比较，从多个维度做出尽可能全面的对比。教师还应补充语言点。文中有关对比的词语有 in contrast、in addition、while、but等，其他常用的还有 similar to、on one hand... on the other hand、in comparison、whereas、however 等。

4）音视频文本

The Impact of Culture on Education

Cultural tendencies impact the way children participate in education. The table below describes different expectations about "normal" school behavior for students from individualist and collectivist cultures. Take a moment to think about how teachers who lack knowledge about culture might interpret the behavior of a child from a collectivist culture. These differences may cause educators to inaccurately judge students from some cultures as poorly behaved or disrespectful. In addition, because cultural differences are hard to perceive, students may find themselves reprimanded by teachers but fail to understand what they did that caused concern.

The influence of culture on beliefs about education, the value of education, and participation styles cannot be overestimated. Many Asian students, for example, tend to be quiet in class, and making eye contact with teachers is considered inappropriate for many of these children. In contrast, most European American children are taught to value active classroom discussion and to look teachers directly in the eye to show respect, while their teachers view students' participation as a sign of engagement and competence.

Another contrast involves the role of Hispanic parents in education. Parents from some Hispanic cultures tend to regard teachers as experts and will often defer educational decision-making to them. In contrast, European American parents are often more actively involved in their children's classrooms, are visible in the classrooms, or volunteer and assist teachers. These cultural differences in values and beliefs may cause educators to make inaccurate judgments regarding the value that non-European American families place on education. While it is important to keep in mind that different cultural groups tend to follow particular language and interaction styles, there is tremendous variability within cultural groups. Thus, educators need to understand individual histories and ideologies regarding education and learning as well as the cultural patterns and beliefs of groups.

5）变化与拓展

这一材料的拓展活动可设计为三分钟演讲，将视听训练和读写训练结合起来。教师可将其布置为课后作业让学生做，演讲则在随后一周的课堂上进行，主题设定为中外教育，具体题目则由学生在一定范围内自拟。学生在课后进行拓展阅读、视听，深入探讨隐藏在现象背后的跨文化因素，再撰写演讲稿。也可采用小组合作的形式完成此项作业。还可选择以中外教育的跨文化对比为主题的纪录片作为课后拓展活动，如观看《中国老师来了》(*The School That Turned Chinese*)，在欣赏影片的同时，增加跨文化知识。

4.4.4 跨文化听力活动设计四：评价听力材料中的跨文化现象

1）要点讲解

　　另一项重要的跨文化技能就是评价，即培养学习者秉持尊重和开放的态度，运用自己的跨文化知识，对所听材料做出有理有据的判断。当我们识别出听力材料中的文化差异时，重要的是做到不要轻易做判断。第一，应承认差异的存在，尊重世界文化的多样性；第二，应努力了解这些差异，寻找证据，思考现象背后的原因；第三，应尝试运用同理心，从他人角度去感受和体验。此外，在看到差异的同时也要去发现共性。总之，我们不应抱有偏见，而应在充分观察、聆听和思考的基础上对跨文化现象做出审慎的评价。

2）课前准备

　　(1) 准备一篇视听材料，应含有可评价的文化现象。本例关注的是中外养老文化的差异。

　　(2) 选择影片《涉外大饭店》中的片段。该片展现了西方"外包式养老"中的跨文化现象。

　　(3) 准备相应的中国文化材料。在此例中，需准备中国文化中对赡养老人的传统看法与做法。这样的设计能帮助学生清楚了解自身文化的出发点，也能达到训练学生利用外语表达中华优秀传统文化的目的。例如，下例是"樊迟问仁"的故事。

When his student Fan Chi asked him about *ren*, Confucius replied, "Love of people." This is Confucius' most important interpretation of *ren*. Love for the people is universal love. Confucius further emphasized that this kind of love should "begin with the love of one's parents." He believed no one could love people in general if they did not even love their own parents. Confucius regarded "filial piety and fraternal duty" as the essence of *ren*. *The Doctrine of the Mean* (*Zhongyong*) quotes Confucius as saying, "The greatest love for people is the love of one's parents." He also said, "Children should not travel far while their parents are alive. If they have no choice but to do so, they must retain some restraint." He did not mean that children should not leave their parents at all. What he meant was that children should not make their parents anxious about them while away from home. Confucius said again, "Children should think often of the age of their parents. They should feel happy for the health and longevity of their parents. They should also feel concern for the aging of their parents."

（选自《大学思辨英语视听说》第 1 册）

3）活动实例

听前

教师需要说明本次活动的重点是在识别文化现象的基础上做出评价。教师与学生对话，询问应怎样做出评价。具体的问题包括：你觉得对待文化差异应抱有怎样的态度？怎样分析文化差异产生的原因？你是否也会关注文化中的共同点？等等。

听中

本听力材料是一篇有关美国老人在家中养老的新闻报道。教师设计的任务如下：

Listen to a news report on looking after elderly people. According to the report, many Americans now choose to look after their elderly family members by themselves, in a paid or unpaid manner. Meanwhile, more and more Chinese are sending their parents to nursing homes, which used to be considered against the tradition. How do you evaluate the phenomena? Discuss in groups and prepare a group presentation of three minutes to illustrate your ideas.

在我们传统的认知中，西方社会与中国社会在赡养老人方面一直有不同的文化习惯。自古中国传统文化提倡孝道，赡养老人是应尽义务，大部分老人在上了年纪后会与子女一起生活，而西方社会中大部分老人或独居或去养老院。然而这篇听力材料则让我们看到，美国中西部一位 94 岁的老人与儿子一家人相伴，还拿出养老金接济经济窘迫的孩子，与中国人的做法颇为相似。这一材料让我们看到了两种文化中的共性。新闻报道中，儿子 David Fowler 说："At first, we were kind of uncomfortable with what he was talking about because…I don't want to make a profit off of my mother. That's just not in our way of thinking." 虽然他夫妻俩经济比较拮据，但是仍愿意无偿照顾高龄的母亲。于是，弟弟提议母亲付一部分退休金给哥哥。就这样，母亲在大儿子家养老，而不是去养老院。一家人都很满意这样的决定。在这篇新闻报道中还有一个朴实感人的细节，就是大儿子打趣母亲说："在家里的孩子中，你最喜欢我了"，而母亲却说"你们几个都这么说，但是我一视同仁，你们都一样好。"

Son：You always loved me best.

Mother：That's what all three of you say. But there's no good, better, or best in this family. You're all best. At least to me.

这一听力材料也许动摇了我们对西方养老方式的刻板印象。同样地，我们反观自己，能够发现中国传统的赡养方式也正在发生改变。养老院的兴起，为有此需求的人提供了选择的可能。我们对养老院的刻板印象也在改变。

听后

教师需要针对学生的回答做总结。首先，在跨文化交际中，我们不能只看到差别，还应看到共性。从本质上说，人类的情感是共通的。文化对比不是只看到不同，还要看到相似或相同点。在客观分析现象背后原因的同时，还应运用同理心去感受和体会。很多学生在做小组汇报时，都重点在分析"美国老人在家养老"和"中国老人去养老院"这两种现象的原因和强调两种文化的差别，未能看到人性中的共性。其次，刻板印象的存在会影响我们对文化现象乃至对社会、经济等各种现象的准确判断。保持客观、独立的思考和判断，注重对时代变化的观察和体验，有助于消除刻板印象。

4）音视频文本

David Fowler and his wife take care of his 94-year-old mother Mary Ruth, a retired teacher. She was widowed in the 1960s and lived on her own until a few years ago. But when her eyesight started failing, they moved her from Indianapolis into their home in Ogallala, Nebraska.

David's preparing his mom an afternoon shot of caffeine.

David Fowler: "Unlike most of the people who come from Indiana, who like colored water, she likes strong coffee."

He heads up to her room on the second floor.

David: "Room service!"

Mary Ruth Fowler: "Oh my goodness!"

David: "There's your espresso."

Mary Ruth: "Very good."

David: "Mmmmmm..."

Mary Ruth: "Mmm-hmm."

Mary Ruth is blind now but she's still pretty self-sufficient. She climbs the stairs and dresses herself, although David and his wife Gloria lay out her clothes. She's started showing signs of dementia, so they've taken her pills into their room and they make sure she takes what she needs when she needs it.

David says it's a joy to care for his mom and he'd do it for free, but he doesn't. Mary Ruth pays her son $1,000 a month. It was his brother's idea.

"At first we were kind of uncomfortable with what he was talking about because...I don't want to make a profit off of my mother. That's just not in our way of thinking."

But the money is welcome. David will soon turn 70. He and Gloria both work part-time. For years they owned a photo studio in town and plowed everything they made back into the business.

"Well, as it turned out, digital really killed the small mom-and-pop portrait studio and our business was worth maybe half of what we had anticipated when we sold it."

Everyone in the family was happy with the payment arrangement. Nothing was put in writing. But elder law attorneys say the family should draw up a formal personal care contract.

Lawyer Howard Krooks says it's a way to protect the older person. There may come a time when they have to go into a nursing home, have very little money left, and should qualify for Medicaid, the government's medical assistance program for poor Americans. But there's a catch.

"The monies that you paid to the family caregiver absent on an agreement in writing will be aimed to have been gifted by you to the family caregiver, causing a period of delay wherein which you will not qualify for the Medicaid benefit."

In other words, Medicaid may not pay for care for months – or even years – because it considers dollars given to a family member money that could have been saved to pay for nursing care. But if both parties sign a contract before the family caregiver starts the job, Medicaid accepts that as an employment agreement.

Howard Krooks says his business in this area has doubled in the last several years. Other elder care lawyers say the same. So why are more families turning a personal relationship into a business arrangement? Krooks points to the recession. Some of his clients are adult children who were laid off and can't find new jobs.

"They find themselves in a position of care-giving and there's a way to really satisfy two needs: the need of the parent for the care – and the parent would have to spend a whole lot more money to hire a third party to provide similar level of services – and the need of the child to be able to earn one's keep."

He says he expects the number of paid family members to keep rising even as the economy recovers, because the need for care-giving is growing as America's population ages.

Of course, money is famous for causing family feuds. Krooks has seen arrangements fall apart because one relative hated the idea.

"They were frankly looking to have another family member provide the services in an unpaid manner, so that more money could be left in the estate, and hopefully when the parent died, they would get more money. And I'm sorry to say that, you know, that's reality."

That's not a problem in the Fowler family. For one thing, there's not much of an estate to leave. For another, everyone gets along – even if David teases his mother about the family hierarchy.

"You always loved me best."

"That's what all three of you say. But there's no good, better, or best in this family. You're all best. At least to me."

They just take on day by day: Enjoying a joke, a glass of wine and each other's company.

5）变化与拓展

这篇听力材料还有一个重要的内容，就是律师 Howard Krooks 从法律角度提醒，如果老人用退休金补贴照顾她的子女，就应签订协议。这样，这笔钱就被视为雇佣护理人的开支，而不是对子女的赠与。因为根据美国法律规定，在申请 Medicaid 的前五年，如果申请人有不当赠与行为，将导致申请资格的批准延期，从而无法及时拿到政府的养老补助。律师还提到了在赡养老人时可能引起的家庭纷争。这一部分在材料中占据的比例超过一半，需要一定的法律常识，有一定难度。因此，拓展活动可以加强对这部分的理解。

第五章　学术听力活动

5.1　学术听力的情境案例

近两年，我在课程中增加了学术听力的内容。这一项安排源于一次教学。在那次课上，我讲了听力认知策略，其中包括笔记策略。我给学生练习的听力材料是一篇有关记忆的学术讲座片段，有9分钟长，比平时听的材料长一些。我在教室里转了一圈，发现多数人没有记笔记，有两三个人拿着笔记本，但是上面也只有零星的几个字，可以看出来并没有记下什么。也许是学生还没有养成记笔记的习惯，也许是讲座里有脑科学方面的生僻词汇，学科内容也较为陌生的缘故。我决定专门安排几周时间，加强学术听力能力的训练。

通过检查和阅读学生的听力笔记，我发现他们的笔记有这样几个特点：1）总体来说能记下来一些内容，但是看不出结构；2）基本上开头部分记得比较好，后面越来越少，或干脆放弃；3）内容显得支离破碎、中断处较多；4）遇到听不懂的词，勉强记下前几个字母，或干脆画上横线。虽然这是没有经过整理的笔记的原貌，但是也反映出笔记技能不足的问题。联想到现在的讲课、讲座大都使用PPT演示文稿，而对于重要内容学生都是用手机直接拍摄，我也就不觉得奇怪了。

是不是我们在听的过程中真的不用做笔记了？我向几个去国外读研的学生了解，他们说学校不允许学生上课时使用手机，所以他们必须记笔记。虽然课后有幻灯资料可以提供，但是老师讲课的很多内容并不在PPT上。他们还说，英语本族语学生的笔记记得非常快，内容非常多。

看来，学习记笔记的技能，尤其对聆听学术语篇，还是颇为必要。记不下来，有学科专业词汇量少的原因，有来不及抓取信息的原因，也有笔记技能不足的原因。那么，应该怎样才能做好听力笔记、提高学术听力水平呢？

学术英语属于专门用途英语（ESP），又可分为通用学术英语和专门用途学术英语（Jordan 1997）。就通用学术英语而言，学术英语能力是指具有听懂英文学术讲座、阅读英文学术文献、撰写英文学术文章、做英文学术报告和参加英文学术讨论的能力。可见，学术英语的使用，除了书面交流，还包括在专业讲座、学术研讨、国际会议等各种学术语境下使用英语进行的口头交流。因此，良好的学术听说能力必不可少。

然而，相比学术阅读和写作，学术英语听和说一直是我国学生的薄弱环节。据国内相关研究，研究生（非英语专业）听不懂英文学术报告、不能流畅地使用英语进行学术对话的情况还很普遍（杨亚丽、杨帆 2014）。钟兰凤和钟家宝（2015）对理工科硕士生的调查发现，87% 的研究生对学术英语有中等及以上的焦虑，高于对通用英语的焦虑。可以说，学术英语是英语学习者普遍面临的一个难点。从高层次人才的培养来说，学术听说能力则是不可或缺而且亟待提高的重要能力。

5.2　学术听力的理论框架

5.2.1　学术听力的定义

国外对学术听说能力的要求最早可以追溯到 20 世纪初。1913 年，剑桥英语证书考试就包含高级听说测试，用来选拔来剑桥大学和牛津大学读书的外国学生。测试为学术导向，包含听写、朗读、对话和书面的语音知识测试，时间长达 90 分钟（Weir 2003）。后来，随着录音技术的普及，从 20 世纪 60、70 年代起，各类重要考试都开始测试听力，其中大都包含学术内容。

学术听力这一概念最初是指听外语讲座，做笔记。在 20 世纪 80、90 年代的课本中，学术听力绝大部分是以教学生做好笔记为主要目标。我国较早研究学术听力的郑仲华（1989：7）认为，学术听力（Academic Listening）就是俗称的"听讲座"，即

学术听力是听力理解中的高级阶段，不同于一般听力理解只简单地要

求理解短文的大意，或辨认词的连续形式，推测词在句中的意思，或划分词与词的界限。它要求听话人要具有独立地理解真实的、正常语速的长篇讲座的能力，能够准确地识别讲座的论题、主题、主要思想与次要思想，迅速流利地写下包含主题、分主题、重要细节和例子等的记录或提纲。它是敏锐的理解能力、准确的判断能力和快速的笔记能力的结合，是一门高级的学术技巧。

这一定义在 20 世纪 90 年代之后得到拓展。Flowerdew & Miller（1997）指出，只注重"听讲座、做笔记"的教材并不能够使外语学习者真正具备听懂外语讲座的能力。通过观察讲座、分析讲座文本、组织师生讨论，两位作者指出，学术听力不能仅以听懂讲座、做好笔记为目标，还应包含对口头语篇特征的掌握、对讲座人采用的人际策略的了解、对学术讲座话语结构的熟悉，等等。

此后，有关学术听力的研究逐渐增多，研究视角不再只是听讲座、记笔记，而是延伸到更多的场合和更多样的交流情境，比如学术会议和学术研讨。发言者既有英语母语使用者，也有非英语母语使用者。这些研究包括对发言人话语韵律的分析（如 Thompson 2003）、笔记对讲座理解的作用（如 Chaudron et al. 1994）、听者对话语线索的利用（如 Jung 2003）、语言水平对学术听力理解的影响（如 Mecartty 2000；Vandergrift 2006）、学术会议视觉展示方式研究（如 Rowley-Jolivet 2002）、讲座人传递信息的方式如手势线索（如 Hood & Forey 2005）、讲座中的师生互动（如 Morell 2004，2007），等等。学术听力的定义得到拓宽，学术听力的范围不仅仅指听讲座，还包括小组讨论、团队合作项目、研讨会、与导师讨论等常见的学术情境，这些活动都涉及对以学术内容为主的语言的感知和理解。此外，学术听力不仅仅指单向听力，也指双向听力（Lynch 2011）。

5.2.2　学术听力的难点

无论是参加国际会议，还是在课堂里听课、研讨，听学术英语对外语学习者来说始终是一个挑战。Rahimirad & Moini（2015）指出，听力难，学术英语听力更难。那么，学术听力的难点到底有哪些？

1）学术听力内容的专业性

首先，学术听力在内容上具有专业性。从学习者的角度看，学术听力的主要目的是获取新的知识和技能，包括学习知识信息、掌握抽象概念、增强概念性理解，等等（Chamot & O'Malley 1994）。因此，要听懂学术语篇，首先要解决专业术语概念理解的问题。虽然专业知识本身并不是外语课堂传授的重点，但是这些知识的外语表达却与外语学习有直接关系，集中表现在专业词汇上。

词汇量不够是二语学习者在学术听力中遇到的主要障碍之一。Kelly（1991）认为，听学术英语听得不好，最主要原因是词汇量不够。众多研究表明，词汇是影响听力理解的首要因素（Stæhr 2009；王艳 2014）。那么，要听懂学术英语，到底需要多少词汇量呢？

在第二章里已经提到，研究表明，对于口头语言，要想达到基本理解，需要有95%的词汇覆盖率，即需要掌握3000个词族加上专有名词和边缘词汇；要想达到充分理解，需要有98%的词汇覆盖率，即需要掌握6000—7000个词族加上专有名词和边缘词汇（Nation 2006；Webb & Rodgers 2009a，2009b）。那么对于学术语言，是不是也要达到这个词汇量？

Dang & Webb（2014）采用BASE语料库对这一问题做了回答。该语料库包括160篇讲座和39篇研讨会录音，采集于英国两所大学，分别来自艺术与人文、生命科学与医学、物理学、社会科学等四个领域。研究发现，4000个词族加上专有名词和边缘词汇，能够达到96.05%的词汇覆盖率；8000个词族加上专有名词和边缘词汇，能够达到98%的词汇覆盖率。该研究指出，要听懂学术英语并达到足够理解，需要大大地增加词汇量。可见，以听懂一般英语的词汇量来听学术英语，显然是不够的。

该研究还指出，词汇量究竟需要增加多少，在不同学科中是不一样的。在社会科学领域，需要3000个词族加上必要的专有名词和边缘词汇来覆盖95%

的学术英语词汇，以及 5000 个词族加上必要的专有名词和边缘词汇来覆盖 98% 的学术英语词汇。但是到了生命科学和医学领域，这两个数字就分别变成 5000 和 13000。在该研究调查的四个领域中，听懂社会科学的讲座，所需要的词汇量最少，而听懂生命科学和医学的讲座，需要的词汇量最大。这里面所包含的学科专门词汇，被称作技术性词汇。

一般来说，不是某个专业领域的学习者，不会花时间去专门学习该专业的技术性词汇。不过，还有一种词汇，在学术英语中出现的频率也非常高，如 approach、assess、assume、derive、interpret、formula、establish、evident、specific 等。有不少语言研究者和教育者发现，令学生最感困难的并非学科所特有的专业词汇，而是这些通用于各个学科，较常出现在学术性文字中，在日常交流中却使用不多的词语。这些词被称为半技术性词汇（陈琦 & 高云 2010）。

在第二章里也已经提到过，词族的数量并不是词汇的个数。那么，上述的词族数量，相当于多少个词汇呢？上文说到，如果我们要求学习者在听学术报告时达到基本理解，他们就需要有 95% 的词汇覆盖率，也就是 3000—4000 个词族加上专有名词和边缘词汇。一般来说，不同使用频率的词族对应的词汇量有相当大的差别。例如，使用频率最高的前 1000 个词族，含有 6857 个不同的词，但随着词汇使用频率的下降，低频词的词族就不会像这样平均每个词族有 6—7 个词了，而是会下降不少（Nation 2012）。根据以上数据，我们保守估计，学习者要想在听学术英语时达到基本理解，词汇量要在 1—1.2 万以上。可见，要想充分听懂学术语篇，词汇量是一个必要条件，而目前我国学习者的学术词汇量缺口依然很大。

2）学术话语的语言特征

基于书面语的研究发现，在语法和词汇上，学术语篇比日常用语更为复杂。在语义层面，学术语篇以密集的学术词汇为特征；在语法层面，学术语篇以被动语态及长而复杂的名词、介词短语、名词化、分词做修饰词为特征（Abedi & Lord 2001；Heller & Morek 2015；Scarcella & Rumberger 2000；Snow & Uccelli 2009。转引自 Marx et al. 2016）。学术话语与之有共性，同时也具有口头语言的特点。

例如，Flowerdew & Miller（1997）指出，学术讲座具有口头语言的特征。与学术文本不同，学术讲座通常按照调群来组建结构，有时句子不完整，还常常会有停顿，使用例如 ah、um 或者 and、so、but、therefore、however 这样的话语标记。这些话语标记在口语中可以用来提示话语的延续、切分或者话题的转换。说话人还时常有错误起句、冗余和重复等现象。这些原本就是自然语言所带有的特点，有时令学术话语不像学术文本那样精确、严谨，也可能给听者带来一些理解上的困难。

Flowerdew & Miller(1997) 还指出，讲座都有一定的话语结构，如古典法、解决问题法、顺序法、对比法、主题法和原因–影响法，等等（Chan 1995）。如果听者熟悉这些话语结构，也就是说如果他们听之前就具备与话语结构相关的知识，那么他们对讲座的理解就会好得多。同时，讲座人通常会利用宏观标记来提示讲座的结构，如果能抓住这些标记，也有助于识别讲座的组织构架。

相比较学术文本，学术话语还有一个特点，就是它还带有人际交往的特征。说话人会采用人际策略来促进交际的成功。再以讲座为例，讲座人经常通过设问句（自己提问、自己回答）或用"我们"做主语来拉近与听者之间的距离，形成讲座人和听者共同构建讲座的效果。他们或争取与听众找到共同点，或通过不断询问听众是否同意来保持不断的接触（Flowerdew & Miller 1997）。讲座人的身势语通常也能对听者的理解起到帮助作用。但是，讲座人的说话风格对听者的理解产生的影响却并不一致。一般而言，讲座人说话的风格有对话型、修辞型、报告型和讨论型（Dudley-Evans 1994）。各种风格对应的难度因人而异，有人觉得对话型生动活泼，容易理解，有人觉得修辞型不容易懂，因为要理解讲座人隐喻性的语言（Littlemore 2001）。总之，不熟悉学术话语的这些语言特征，就难以摸着学术听力的门道。

3）学术话语情境下的多重任务

在学术听力场合，听者常常面临多重任务。从内容上说，听者不但需要运用语言知识进行理解，还需要运用专业知识进行思考。用本族语理解这些学科知识点就不容易，更何况使用外语。因此，认知负担不可谓不重。同时，从信息交流渠道上看，常常是听、写、读、说同时进行。以学术研讨为例，参与者常常需要阅读书面材料上或屏幕投影上的文字、图表或图片资料，聆听其他人发言，聆听或观看通过多媒体呈现的音视频资料，时常需要做笔记，还需要参与讨论。总之，听者在学术听力中需要对抗多重任务同时进行而带来的压力（Arnold 2000），这对于二语学习者来说，也是一个不小的挑战。

5.3 学术听力的教学目标

基于前面对学术听力的定义和对学术听力难点的分析，我们不难发现，学术听力除了具有一般听力的属性，还具有其自身的特点。

第一，学术听力的专业性强。这一难点表现为学术听力中常常含有大量的技术性词汇和半技术性词汇。学术听力的认知要求高，同时信息比较抽象，没有紧密的语境配合，讲座人和听者之间可共享的知识较少（Marx et al. 2016）。第二，学术话语在语言上呈现一定的规律性。它具有口头语言中的话语标记，也具有常用的话语结构，还带有人际交往的不同风格。第三，学术听力过程中往往伴随多重任务。这些特点交织在一起，使学术听力成为一大难点。基于此，学术听力课堂可设立以下的教学目标。

5.3.1 加强学术词汇学习

提高词汇量是提高英语学术听力能力的最重要途径。学术词汇不仅指与学科相关的专业词汇，还包括学术领域通用的一些专门词汇，它们当中有不少属于较难掌握的低频词。对于词汇，不但应该看得懂，还应该听得懂。也就是说，应全面掌握学术词汇的音、形、义，才能保证其在学术交流场合的准确运用。课堂上应着重在两个方面展开学术词汇教学：一是积累词汇，即帮助学习者掌握扩大词汇量的方法；二是在线处理生词，即帮助学习者掌握遇到生词时的处理策略。

5.3.2　识别学术话语的基本结构

　　学术话语特有的体裁、推理方式和论证策略，以及说话人的风格等，使不同场合的学术话语形成了一定的规律性特征。无论是讲座还是研讨会，如果熟悉它的结构和体裁，那将能帮助听者预测讲座或会话的进展，极大地帮助理解。因此，熟练识别和判断学术话语的体裁和结构是学术听力教学的目标之一。可以以单向学术听力和双向学术听力为两个重点，以其各自常见的体裁举例，展示常见的结构，同时选取不同类型的说话人风格，让学生对比分析，掌握其特点。

5.3.3　识别学术话语标记或线索

　　学术听力的另一个教学目标是识别学术话语的标记或线索。在学术讲座这样的单向听力活动中，因为没有机会或者很少有机会与说话人交流，所以听力理解主要依赖听懂话语本身，那么它们所携带的标记或者线索就显得格外重要。另一方面，讲座人也常常会主动给予听众提示，希望听众能像自己一样，条理清晰地把握所讲内容的结构。讲座的话语线索一般分为两类，一类是元话语线索，一类是语调线索（Thompson 2003）。对于其他类型的学术听力，基本也可以从文本和韵律这两类线索入手，设计教学活动。

5.3.4　综合运用听力策略

　　积极有效地运用听力策略，可降低多重任务压力。例如，采用元认知策略中的计划策略，将注意力集中在最为重要的部分；采用联想、推断、做笔记等认知策略，促进听力理解；采用合作策略，有不懂的地方及时向同伴提问。总之，可训练学生采用多种策略，积极主动应对学术听力活动中可能产生的困难。其中，笔记策略具有重要的地位。几乎每个人都有过使用笔记策略来记录要点、帮助理解和记忆的经历，但是绝大多数人并没有掌握行之有效的记笔记方法。这一策略可以作为教学的目标之一。

5.4 学术听力教学设计实例

这一部分针对教学目标分别设计了学术听力教学活动。与前面的章节一样，每个教学活动先讲解相应的知识点，再建议可准备的材料和活动形式，并给出活动实例、材料文本，以及活动的变化和拓展建议。

5.4.1 学术听力活动设计一：学术词汇"听中学"

1）要点讲解

前文已经说明，要听懂学术英语并达到充分理解，需要拥有比较大的词汇量。而且，对一个单词的音、形、义要掌握全面，才能形成熟练的匹配，即听到词的音就知道意思，在需要做笔记的时候，也能拼写出来。这要求我们对词汇教学的重要性要有足够的认识，并切实地体现在教学设计中。

学术词汇往往比较抽象，有在意思上容易混淆的词，还有不少的多音节词。在实际教学中，学生常常有两种反应，一是"似曾相识，但一下子想不起来"，二是"完全不懂"。前者极有可能是遇到了"看得懂却听不懂"的词汇，应着重加强音-义的关联，将这种部分掌握的词汇转化为全面掌握的词汇；对完全陌生的词汇，建议从音的记忆开始，采取音-义-形的步骤学习。

我们还要教会学生在"听中学"。要达到1万以上的词汇量，需要较长时间的积累。在学习的过程中，遇到生词是常态。这时，猜词策略有一定的帮助。比较常用的是利用词缀和上下文来猜词。需要注意的是，这些方法源于阅读理解，而在听力理解中，听者完全靠听音来判断，而且没有机会重复听，所以猜词策略并不是轻易就能奏效。需要集中注意力，基于语境充分展开联想。建议在听完材料之后，无论猜对猜错，都不要将生词随意放过，可通过重听、看文本、查字典、询问他人等多种办法，学习这个词。这一方法不仅适用于学术词汇的学习，还适用于其他词汇的学习。应尽早尽快提高词汇量。

2）课前准备

（1）准备学术听力材料一篇，确保其中含有某个学科的专门词汇；

（2）将文中用于教学的目标生词挑选出来，标记位置或剪辑成短音频，便于反复播放。同时，设计巩固音–义–形搭配的练习；

（3）准备思维导图的绘制示例，以其中的关键学术词汇为核心，联想更多相近的词汇。

3）活动实例

本例是一个介绍积极心理学的学术访谈，涉及的心理学词汇有 gratitude、accomplishment、optimistic、pessimistic、emotion 等，也有 schizophrenia、cardiovascular、immune 这样的医学词汇，还有普通的专有名词如 Philadelphia（费城）、Bosnia（波斯尼亚）、Danes（丹麦人）以及 Brits（英国人）。此外，catastrophe 是中等难度的词汇，但是多次出现；forbear 仅出现一次，但是在词汇等级上已是属于 1 万词以上的低频词。该访谈内容的学术性和逻辑性较强，句式较长，有一定难度。这里介绍两个听前的词汇练习设计和两个听后的词汇练习设计供参考。

听前设计 1

在听前，先让学生听含有生词解释的句子，如下面这些句子。学生能够学习到这些词的发音和释义。这些句子稍后显示在幻灯上。

- **Cardiovascular** diseases are a group of disorders of the heart and blood vessels.

- **Catastrophic** means involving or causing sudden great damage or suffering.

- **Gratitude** refers to the feeling of being grateful and wanting to express your thanks.

- **Immune** system refers to the system in your body that produces substances to help it fight against infection and disease.

- **Mentality** refers to the particular attitude or way of thinking of a person or group.

学习之后，让学生从以上的词汇中选择合适的词，完成下列句子填空。

- The effects of global warming, while not immediate, are potentially _____.
- Smoking places you at serious risk of _____.
- Despite anything the science of medicine may have achieved, the _____ is our main defense against disease.
- I just cannot understand the _____ of these teenagers.
- I'm writing this letter to express our _____ to you for we have all benefited from the lecture you gave last week.

在这个听前练习中，学生听入词或词组的发音，用英文理解它们的意思，在大脑中形成词义和发音的匹配。句子显示在屏幕上后，学生还能看到词的拼写。这样，学习了音–义–形之后，再完成填空练习。这一练习的目的是通过在语境中使用词汇，以加深记忆。

听前设计 2

听前预习词汇时，还可以采用头脑风暴法。教师抛出一个紧扣听力材料主题的关键词或者问题，让学生说出此刻浮现在大脑中的相关词汇。例如，此例中可以抛出关键词"psychology"或提问"If you hear the term *positive psychology*, what words would pop into your mind?"。当学生你一言我一语说出相关词汇时，教师可选择与目标词汇相近的进行重复；当学生过于偏离主题时，教师可从旁引导、纠正方向。这一活动的好处是学生高度参与，课堂气氛活跃。在大家集思广益地预测可能听到的词汇时，背景知识也得到了激活。

听后设计 1

可以采用思维导图来做词汇练习。例如，在此例中，可在听完之后学习语言点的时候，采用思维导图梳理刚刚听到的词汇（包括生词）。可以让学生自己画图，也可以完成教师提前准备好的导图填空，如下图：

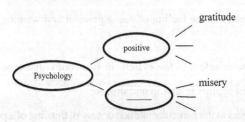

图 5.1　思维导图式词汇填空

听后设计2

还可采用其他方式的听后练习来加强学术词汇学习。学术词汇中很多是表达抽象概念的名词或形容词，如本例中有 spirituality、gratitude、accomplishment、mentality、superficial、intellectual 这样的技术性或半技术性词汇。可设计书面或口头的词性转换、近义词或反义词练习，来加深理解和记忆。

4）音视频文本

Psychologists told us a lot about misery and suffering and drug addiction and schizophrenia, but there's one that's just half-baked. Being a full-baked, what we want to know is what makes life worth living. How about positive emotion? How about meaning? How about spirituality? How about gratitude? How about accomplishment? So, the intellectual idea was for psychology to make full sense of the human condition.

In many circumstances the data are that optimistic people get depressed only half the rate when setbacks occur, that optimistic people do better than expected on the sports field, in grades, and in many kinds of work, that optimistic people have yeastier immune systems, they're less likely to die of cardiovascular diseases and that descriptively optimistic people are generally liked better. It turns out if you take pessimistic people, depressive people which I'm an example, and you teach them principles of recognizing the catastrophic thoughts they're saying to themselves, "This interview was going terribly. I have really lost my touch", and then arguing against it, "No! You know Joe's been laughing and smiling at my jokes throughout", then it turns out you can make people permanently, lastingly more optimistic.

(The) last evolutionary epoch was the Ice Age and the mentality that said, "You know it's a lovely day in Philadelphia today. It'll probably be a lovely day tomorrow" got crushed by the ice, and the mentality that was a catastrophe, "looks like a lovely day in Philadelphia today, but this is just superficial, what's really coming (is a) catastrophe" is what our intellectual evolutionary forbears, the ones that survived, gave us, so we're bad weather animals, ready to see the most catastrophic. Now that's very adaptive if you're in Bosnia during a war, or if you live in a society in which there's death and famine and plague.

One of my colleagues Felicia Huppert has done a massive survey of the 23 European Union nations, and she asked the question in each of these 23 nations: What percentage of adults are flourishing? The criteria for flourishing are high amount of positive emotion, good relationships, high amount of meaning in life, high amount of engagement at work. And by those criteria involving at least 2,000 people in every nation, 32 percent of Danes are flourishing, (and) 15 percent of Brits are flourishing. Only five percent of Russians are flourishing.

What is (the) positive psychology and well-being's long-term goal? Well, I called it 51. It is the notion that by these criteria, of high positive emotion, high engagement, high meaning, good relationships, in the year 2051, 51 percent of the world's population will be flourishing. Now that's a grandiose dream and I don't know how it will happen, but we've now been able to define the notion of flourishing. We know quite a bit about what increases positive emotion, engagement, meaning, and I think it's a great vision for the future of my science and my discipline to be part of a movement that creates vastly more flourishing around the world.

5）变化与拓展

在学术听力课程的开始，可先测试学生的学术词汇量，并指导每个人设定可行的目标，在课程结束时检验是否达到。也可开展一些小竞赛，激发学生对学术词汇的学习兴趣。重复有利于记忆，应尽可能多地提供生词的语音输入，给学生创造多次听到这个词的机会，并设计说或者写的活动让学生使用这些刚学到的学术词汇。

5.4.2 学术听力活动设计二：识别讲座的结构

1）要点讲解

讲座的结构与讲座的内容、目的和讲座人的风格等是分不开的。一般来说，独立话题的讲座经常采用介绍背景、提出问题、给出解决方案、做出评价这样的框架，而一门课程中的系列讲座则更注重每个讲座之间的关联，如会先回顾上一讲的内容，再从某一点接下来继续展开，结尾的时候还会预告下一讲的内容。

总体来说，讲座可分为开头、主体和结尾部分。开头部分包括开场白、介绍背景和结构；主体部分一般信息量最大，时间较长，通常包括观点、论据、论证过程，等等；结尾部分通常为回顾、总结和展望，有时还会抛出思考性的问题。讲座结构也有不同的样式。例如，大纲式的讲座在一开头就会把主题分几个部分，那么讲座主体就是依次剖析每个部分；案例式的讲座在开头部分会描绘案例情境、提出案例问题，在主体部分则是分析案例和解决问题，在结尾部分给出评价。还有的讲座以时间为线索，如有关历史沿革的主题。

幽默风趣的演讲人可能会通过穿插故事、玩笑、提问来拉近与听众的距离，结构也许不紧密，但是内容吸引力强；循规蹈矩的演讲人按部就班地陈述，也许略显枯燥但是结构清晰、容易理解。因此，严格地说，讲座并没有完全固定的样式。我们可以做到的，是通过对不同结构讲座的聆听，熟悉讲座的常见结构，掌握其中的规律。例如，从开头部分推断讲座的缘由或背景，预测讲座的大体内容；在主体部分，听清讲座人传达的知识要点或观点，识别下定义、分类、对比、例证、因果等论证方法；在结尾部分，听懂讲座人的回顾、总结或建议。学习者掌握了这些结构知识，就能够通过"自上而下"的方式弥补自己在"自下而上"处理中的不足。

2）课前准备

（1）准备多篇具有不同结构的听力材料，用作对比。

（2）将听力材料的结构提前做好图表，同时准备一份让学生填写的表格，内含演讲者姓名、题目、领域、主题、目的、观点等，作为练习让学生听后填写。

(3) 将教学所聚焦部分的结构总结出来，做成问题供听力练习。

3）活动实例

听前

本次课堂教学的目的是让学生通过比较，了解不同听力材料具有不同的结构，同时也要明白无论是什么结构，各部分都是为整体服务。教师可选择两篇听力材料的开头部分，让学生在对比中学会识别。一篇是 TED 演讲，话题为教育，演讲人为 Ken Robinson，题为"如何逃出教育的死亡谷"(How to Escape Education's Death Valley)，演讲旨在指出西方教育中存在的问题。另一篇选自麻省理工学院的系列讲座课程"计算机科学及编程导论"(Introduction to Computer Science and Programming)，演讲者为 Eric Grimson。此讲座为系列讲座中的第二讲。听前，教师询问学生，TED 演讲和专业课讲座在篇章结构上是否有区别，有哪些区别。

听中

先让学生们把两篇材料各听一遍。教师提问以下问题：

• Why does the speaker, Sir Ken Robinson, mention "Americans don't get irony" in the beginning part of the lecture? Is it relevant?

• Can you predict the main theme of this TED talk?

• What does Professor Grimson want to say to his students in the beginning part of his lecture?

• What do "diving into the nitty-gritty" and "the nuts and bolts of the basics of computation" mean?

两个材料的开头部分形成鲜明对比。TED 演讲是一个独立成篇的演讲。演讲人 12 年前从英国搬来美国，他便用自己的经历开头，一边调侃，一边切入正题，演讲轻松自然，听众笑声不断。第二个讲座是大学讲堂中的系列课程，教授也试图用一两句小幽默来活跃气氛，吸引学生的注意，但是非常简短，几乎是立刻转入课程讲解。在简要回顾了上一节内容之后，教授对本节课要讲的内容做了介绍。

听后

教师在听后总结时要提醒学生，虽然同为演讲，但是目的不同、听众不同，其结构也不一样。TED 演讲中使用了幽默风趣的开头，看似与主旨不太关联，但是当出现"No Child Left Behind"（"不让一个孩子落后"——美国的一项教育计划）时，听者则不免会心一笑。讲座人颇费心思的铺垫，实际上已经清楚地点出演讲的主旨，即指出美国教育存在的方向性错误。而"计算机科学及编程导论"的开头是典型的大学课程讲课方式。讲座人不断说明的是本讲内容与上一讲和今后讲座的关系，即之前的内容比较宽泛，而本次讲座开始讨论细节，还有一些会在今后再讨论。这样开头的主要目的，是使听众明确本讲在整个体系中的位置。

4）音视频文本

(1) How to Escape Education's Death Valley

Thank you very much!

I moved to America 12 years ago with my wife Terry and our two kids. Actually, truthfully, we moved to Los Angeles (*laughter*) thinking we were moving to America. But anyway, it's a short plane ride from Los Angeles to America.

I got here 12 years ago, and when I got here, I was told various things, like, "Americans don't get irony." Have you come across this idea? It's not true. I've traveled the whole length and breadth of this country. I have found no evidence that Americans don't get irony. It's one of those cultural myths, like, "The British are reserved." I don't know why people think this. We've invaded every country we've encountered. (*laughter*) But it's not true Americans don't get irony, but I just want you to know that that's what people are saying about you behind your back. You know, so when you leave living rooms in Europe, people say, thankfully, nobody was ironic in your presence.

But I knew that Americans get irony when I came across that legislation No Child Left Behind. Because whoever thought of that title gets irony, don't they? Because (*laughter, applause*) because it's leaving millions of children behind. Now I can see that's not a very attractive name for legislation: Millions of Children Left Behind. I can see that. What's the plan? Well, we propose to leave millions of children behind, and here's how it's going to work.

And it's working beautifully. In some parts of the country, 60 percent of kids drop out of high school. In the native American communities, it's 80 percent of kids. If we halved that number, one estimate is it would create a net gain to the US economy over 10 years of nearly a trillion dollars. From an economic point of view, this is good math, isn't it, that we should do this? It actually costs an enormous amount to mop up the damage from the dropout crisis.

But the dropout crisis is just the tip of an iceberg. What it doesn't count are all the kids who are in school but being disengaged from it, who don't enjoy it, who don't get any real benefit from it.

And the reason is not that we're not spending enough money. America spends more money on education than most other countries. Class sizes are smaller than in many countries. And there are hundreds of initiatives every year to try and improve education. The trouble is, it's all going in the wrong direction. There are three principles on which human life flourishes, and they are contradicted by the culture of education under which most teachers have to labor and most students have to endure.

The first is this, that human beings are naturally different and diverse.

(2) Introduction to Computer Science and Programming: An Excerpt

OK, to work. A word of warning: fasten your seat belt. Or another way of saying it is, I'm going to open up the fire hose a little bit today. Last lecture, you might have thought this was a SHASS class. It sounds like a philosophy class, and it was important to set the stage for what we're going to talk about. We talked about very high level things, the notion of recipes, the notion of computation, why you want to do this, what you're going to learn. Today, we're going to dive into the nitty-gritty, the nuts and bolts of the basics of computation and in particular, what I am going to do today is, I'm going to talk about operators and operands, which we did a little bit real last time, in particular, how to create expressions. I'm going to talk about statements as the key building blocks for writing code, and I'm going to introduce simple set of programs and in particular, I'm going to talk about branching, conditionals, and iteration. So, a lot to do. OK?

So, let me jump straight to it. At the end of last lecture, we started introducing some of the pieces you want to do. And I want to remind you of our goal. We are trying to describe processes. We want to have things that deduce new kinds of information. We want to write programs to do that.

If we're going to write programs, we need at least two things. We need some representation for fundamental data, and we saw last time two examples of that. And the second thing we're going to need, is we're going to need a way to give instructions to the computer, to manipulate that data. We need to give it a description of the recipe. In terms of primitive data, what we saw were two kinds, right? Numbers and strings. A little later on in the lecture, we're going to introduce a third kind of value, but what we're going to see through the terms is, no matter how complex a data structure we create, we're going to create a variety of data structures. Fundamentally all of them have their basis, their atomic level if you like, are going to be some combinations of numbers, of strings, and the third type, which are Booleans, which I'm going to introduce a little later on in this lecture.

5）变化与拓展

　　课堂时间有限，而讲座往往比较长，因此教师可将开头、主体和结尾部分分别进行对比。或者，教师将两篇的对应部分剪辑下来，合成在一个视频中。要提醒学生养成关注讲座开头的好习惯。训练有素的讲座人通常善于利用开头吸引听众，因此重要的背景、主旨或者与结构有关的信息会在此出现。讲座人的幽默小故事需要听众有共同的背景才能充分理解，这对于学外语的学生来说反而是难点。可提醒学生，如果没有听懂，也不要背包袱，应及时调整，早点做好进入正题的听讲准备。

5.4.3　学术听力活动设计三：识别讲座中的话语线索

1）要点讲解

前文已提到，讲座中的话语线索可分为韵律线索和文本线索。在自然语速的语流中，升调、降调、停顿等韵律线索有时并不明显，容易忽略，因此需要多听，掌握规律，方能形成语感。韵律特征方面的规律性线索包括讲座人的音调、音高、响度、节奏及其变化。此外，语速变化、停顿等也常常成为帮助理解的线索。比如，讲座人使用升调表示疑问、询问或者句子尚未完成；讲座人用停顿、减慢语速或重读某个词，来强调重点，吸引听众注意。

相对于韵律线索而言，文本线索更为显性，可以通过熟记来加强识别。这种线索是指讲座人使用的一些词或者词组，用来连接自己的观点，表明自己的态度或者组织讲座的结构（Goh 2013），又被称为话语标记。话语标记可以分为宏观标记和微观标记。宏观标记如"I want you to know that…""Back to what we are talking about…""What can we conclude from this?"，分别可用来强调重点、跟在题外话之后切回主题以及提示概括等作用。在讲座或学术研讨中，开头、结尾、描述、比较、对比、下定义、分类、阐述因果、提供论据、举例、列举、总结等，都有常用的宏观标记。微观标记使句子之间的衔接更为紧密，如介词、连词或副词，当然也包括动词、名词等其他词类或者词组。例如，so、well、however可用来表示句子之间的关系。有研究表明，注意这些话语线索有助于对学术语篇的理解和回忆（Jung 2003）。这里以文本线索的识别为例介绍一个活动。

2）课前准备

（1）选择一篇讲座，找到宏观标记和微观标记，标明合适的位置，以便在练习中暂停，用来让学生练习预测下文；

（2）将讲座的文本准备好，挑选需要练习的宏观标记或微观标记，用下划线替代，做成填空练习。

（3）将讲座文本中的主要句群（含有宏观或微观标记的）分离出来并标上数字序号，然后打乱次序，让学生在听时按照文中顺序排序。

（4）将文中的宏观标记和微观标记根据功能进行分类。

3）活动实例

听前

这是一篇有关压力的心理学讲座。听前，教师化身为学术讲座人，用 3 分钟做一个迷你小讲座，说一说为什么压力是一个重要话题。教师稍加夸张地利用音高、响度、语速变化、停顿等韵律特征，以及宏观和微观的话语标记，让学生听出来自己是在给他们韵律线索和文本线索。讲完后，让学生体会哪些线索有助于他们理解。

听中

教师将这个讲座播放 1—2 遍，并要求学生在听的时候注意韵律线索和文本线索，适当记录。听后，教师显示文本，请学生回答他们听到的线索，并将线索高亮表示。本材料中最明显的线索是列举分论点。我们听到"The first thing that most psychologists suggest is…""The second very important way to deal with stress is…" 和 "The third thing psychologists suggest should be done to reduce stress is…"，这些话语标记其实最受听者青睐，不但点明了结构，还便于记笔记。此外，每个分论点中还有其他的线索。例如，我们可以听到 and、or、but、so that、because 等词，是用来表示并列、转折、结果、原因的微观标记。它们传达着句子内部或者句子之间的逻辑关系。

听后

除了总结微观标记，还可总结学术讲座中常用的宏观话语线索，如在讲座开头引入、下定义、举例、描述过程、列举、分类、论证、总结、结尾，等等。布置课后作业，让同学们根据自己听的其他材料，补充更多的话语标记。

4）音视频文本

The first thing that most psychologists suggest is to learn…to recognize…your own stress signals. OK and we all have different types of stress signals, but individuals should monitor themselves for stress signals so that they can focus on minimizing or acknowledging the stress before it gets out of control…and common early signs for many people include irritability…uh insomnia, weight loss, weight gain, smoking, drinking, increases in small or "dumb" errors, tension, tightness of breath, all kinds of things that people get which could be an early signal of stress, and if you're aware of *your* early signs of stress…and as I said people might have *different* early signs of stress. You can consider ways of protecting yourself when you start seeing these signs coming on…so you might decide to withdraw from a stressful situation… or uh reward yourself with equal amounts of low-stress activity time. But once you recognize the stress signals, you can do something to prevent them from getting out of hand…so that's really the first important way to deal with stress appropriately.

The second very important way to deal with stress is to pay attention to your body demands. Most psychologists are finding that a good exercise program, good nutrition, decrease the amount of stress or the effect of stress on the body, in the mind, and this seems quite apparent because exercise can provide a stress-free environment away from your usual stressors, and it keeps your body busy and preoccupied with non-stressful things.

OK…uh…the third thing that psychologists suggest should be done to reduce stress is to make plans and act…when appropriate…and I'll get back to that "when appropriate" comment, OK? But what they suggest is rather than wasting energy on worrying…an individual can direct his or her energy to plan the steps and act, and often just the planning of the action helps reduce the stress because it reduces the worrying and also the results of the plans or actions may serve to remove or weaken the original cause of the stress.

（改编自《朗文英语讲座听力》，勒博布 2006）

5）变化与拓展

教师可让学生做 3—5 分钟学术讲座且使用必要的语篇线索，以帮助听者理解。此活动可布置为家庭作业，在后一周来课堂展示。

教师需要提醒学生的是，除非专门的练习，平时听讲座并不需要刻意去注意所有的话语线索，这样做不必要，也做不到。通常，听主旨和重要细节才是理解的主要目的。

5.4.4　学术听力活动设计四：学会记笔记

1）要点讲解

记笔记一直被认为是一种有效的策略，它既能存储信息用于后期提取，又能深化对信息的加工。记笔记也是二语学习者在听学术讲座时普遍采用的策略。然而，有关笔记的研究结论实际上并不一致。一些研究认为，笔记对整体的听力表现并没有显著的影响。例如，Clark 等（2013）就发现，在听力理解测试中是否允许学生做笔记，对他们的测试表现并没有什么影响。但是，也有一些研究发现，记笔记在某些情况下还是有用的。例如，如果只能听一遍，那么记笔记就能帮助听者抓取一些信息，从而可以减轻大脑的负担。否则，听者必须一直努力去记忆这些信息，使之不被忘记，这样做将占有很多记忆资源。还有研究发现，当听力材料的语速很快的时候，做笔记对听力理解有显著的预测作用，而语速慢的时候则没有（Lin 2006）。另外，所听的话题不同，是否做笔记的影响也不同。听人文类的听力材料时，做笔记比不做笔记有显著的益处；而听物理学的材料，做与不做笔记，则没有什么显著不同（Carrell et al. 2002）。

尽管如此，在听讲座或做研讨等学术场合，做笔记仍然是学生应倚重的策略。他们希望有熟练的笔记技能来记下所有想记下的内容。事实上，一边听外语讲座一边记笔记并不是一件轻松的事。这是因为，听力理解已经占用了相当大的认知资源。我们认为，在时间和注意力均十分有限的情况下，能有选择、有条理地记下说话人的主旨和重要细节，是一项需要训练的技能。

怎样才算会做笔记呢？是把所听到的都记下来，还是只记下自己认为重要的内容？是记下整句还是信息点或关键词？是否需要用缩写或符号？实际上，记录效率才是最重要的。有研究表明，在理解能力、学科知识、工作记忆、注意力和记录效率（Transcription Fluency）等众多因素中，记录效率能够最好地预测笔记的质量（Peverly & Sumowski 2012）。这一研究针对的是母语学生，而二语学生遇到的情况更为复杂，因为他们在理解外语时，并不像母语学生那样已经自动化。二语学生首先要花费较多的时间来听懂，而且拼写上也不总是很熟练。怎样才能提高记录效率？很显然，不需要记录所有内容，没有必要，也很难做到；记信息点或关键词比记整句好；可以使用缩写或符号来代替文字，以节省时间。另一点值得注意的是，课后需要整理笔记，复原完整的信息。

2）课前准备

(1) 将常用的符号示例做成幻灯。例如：表示因果关系可用（∵，∴）；表示并列关系（+）；表示相等、相同（=）；表示不等或不同（≠）；表示正确或肯定（✓）；表示错误或否定（×）；表示增加（↑）；表示减少（↓）；表示结果（→）；表示原因（←）；表示属于（∈）；表示重要性（*，可增加星号个数来表示程度）；表示警示或注意（!，可增加感叹号个数来表示程度）；在存疑的地方可用问号（?）；在主旨处可用（☆），等等。

(2) 将常用词的缩写示例做成幻灯。例如：工业（ind）、农业（agr）、政治（pol）、经济（eco）、贸易（td）、信息（info）、旅游（tv）、税收（tx）、财政（fz）、公司（co.）、新闻（nz）、教育（edu）、举例（e.g.）、开头（intro）、词汇（vocab）、语法（gra）、中国（CN）、美国（US），等等。

(3) 在准备用作笔记练习的听力材料中插入停顿，也可在课堂播放听力材料时手动暂停，但是备课时需提前做好定位。

3）活动实例

听前

本例是一篇有关世界各国幸福指数的研究报告，里面含有概念、数字和有关此项研究结论的事实陈述，学术名词比较抽象，长句也较多，但是它的内容在结构上比较工整，适合用来做笔记的练习。听前，教师用课前准备好的幻灯，介绍常用的符号和缩写，让学生提前熟悉。

听中

为本次听力活动设置的问题如下：

- What is this news program about?
- How is the geography of happiness presented in this latest report?
- What is the difference in points between the ten happiest countries and the least happy countries in terms of average life evaluations?
- How many key factors are mentioned in the news report? What are the three most important ones?

这些问题中有的询问主旨，有的询问细节。可将问题打印好，先发给学生，让他们在听前稍做准备。同时发一张用来做笔记的白纸。练习中，在播放第一遍时，可在每小段结束后预留 5—10 秒给学生对笔记做快速整理，第二遍则不需要。之后的其他练习可慢慢过渡到不留时间，让记笔记与聆听听力材料同步进行。

在学习做笔记的最初阶段，教师应在黑板上展示做笔记的全过程。例如，针对这一篇，可这样做笔记：

Para 1：1st WHR in 2012; WHR in 2013 ↗ interests; readership: 1.5 mil, 50% > 1st WHR；

Para 2：2015 report, by a map of 10 colors; 0 → 10；Top: 7.5，bot: 3; 4=10 happiest-10 least;

Para 3：6 factors: GDP/capita, healthy yrs of life exp., social support, trust, pcvd freedom, generosity.

听后

教师提醒学生，记笔记也需要耗费一定的认知资源，所以应平衡好专心去听与迅速去写之间的关系。不要因为记笔记而分神，导致跟不上快速的语流，影响理解。更不要试图把每个句子每个词都记下来。最后，教师将文本显示在屏幕上，让学生核对自己是否抓住了重点。

4）音视频文本

The world has come a long way since the first World Happiness Report in 2012. Happiness is increasingly considered a proper measure of social progress and a goal of public policy. The first World Happiness Report was published in support of the April 2, 2012 United Nations High Level Meeting on Happiness and Well-Being. The data and analysis in the World Happiness Report 2013 have helped to satisfy, and perhaps to fuel, growing public interest in applying the science of happiness to public affairs. Readership thus far is about 1.5 million, 50% more than for the first World Happiness Report. That interest in turn encouraged a number of local and national experiments in measuring and improving happiness, as well as the production of the World Happiness Report 2015.

In this latest report, the geography of happiness is presented first by means of a map using 10 different colors to show how average 2012 – 2014 life evaluations differ across the world. Average life evaluations, where 0 represents the worst possible life and 10 the best possible, range from an average above 7.5 at the top of the rankings to below 3 at the bottom. A difference of four points in average life evaluations separates the ten happiest countries from the ten least happy countries.

Three-quarters of the differences among countries, and also among regions, are accounted for by differences in six key variables, each of which digs into a different aspect of life. The six factors are GDP per capita, healthy years of life expectancy, social support as measured by having someone to count on in times of trouble, trust as measured by a perceived absence of corruption in government and business, perceived freedom to make life decisions, and generosity as measured by recent donations, adjusted for differences in income. Differences in social support, incomes and healthy life expectancy are the three most important factors, with their relative importance depending on the comparison group chosen.

5）变化与拓展

　　记笔记具有个性化的特征。不必要求学生背下固定的缩写或符号，相反，应鼓励他们自行创造。只要自己熟悉这些记录方式，可以高效率地使用即可。

　　刚开始听的时候，我们并不知道所听材料的结构，只有听完后才能整理出来。所以，可以教会学生怎样在纸上划分区域，留出空白。可以介绍一些常用的笔记方法，如康奈尔笔记法。

第六章 欣赏型听力活动

6.1 欣赏型听力的情境案例

"看英文电影真的能提高听力吗？"

这个问题既被学生问过，也被教师同行问过。我的回答是："能提高"。但是同时我也有点纳闷，为什么他们会怀疑这个被证明（至少是被我自己证明）是千真万确的事情呢？

于是我去问一位学生。她回答说："我也不知道能不能提高听力，因为我感觉我基本上是在看剧情，没怎么关注语言。但是，语感肯定变好了。有语言环境。"

另一名学生说："我觉得也许有点用。不过，我都是开着字幕看的。"

"什么样的字幕？中文还是英文？"我问。

"肯定是中文字幕。要是双语字幕的话，也基本上看中文。"

"那你们还记不记得看电影学到了哪些词汇？"

"暂时想不起来了。"

在一次研讨会上，一位同行问起了同样的问题，我给出了肯定的答复。我告诉她我自己教过的一位研究生，本科是计算机系的，后来考上英语语言学研究生。他的英语表达非常自然、流畅。他说他喜欢英语，学英语就靠追剧。我还告诉这位老师，我自己也会在去上班的地铁上用手机看英文电影，提前把大脑转换到英文频道。

听了我的回答，她还有些将信将疑。她说她也建议过学生课后看英文电影，因为课堂上肯定没有那么多时间。学生们应该也回去看了，但是有没有提高听力就不知道了。

那么到底看英文电影是不是学习听力的好方法呢？

听的目的有多种，娱乐欣赏就是其中之一。听外语歌、看外语影片，都带有娱乐和欣赏的目的。不过，人们发现，这样的活动似乎对外语学习，特别是听力学习有促进作用。我们常常听到成功的外语学习者介绍自己通过听外语歌曲、看外文影视剧来学习外语的经验。甚至还有人说，是一首外文歌点燃了他学习外语的激情。多年来，听歌、看原版电影也一直是外语课堂上最受学生欢迎的活动。

改革开放初期，大量外文歌曲进入中国，带来了异域文化，其中不少经典歌曲受到外语学习者的喜爱。20 世纪 80 年代后期，原版影片也进入了课堂。当时，无论是歌曲、影片资料还是录放音设备，都是稀缺资源。外语系学生上课有机会学外语歌、看外语电影，都成了其他系学生羡慕的事情。如今，随着互联网和移动通信的普及，外语歌曲、电影、电视剧资源已经变得非常容易获得，听歌、追剧已经是稀松平常的事。如果说，从前这么做更多是为了学习，那现在更多是为了欣赏和娱乐。那么以这样的目的，是否也能促进语言学习？应该怎样利用欣赏型活动促进听力学习？本章就将聚焦有关欣赏型听力课堂活动的设计。

6.2　欣赏型听力的理论框架

6.2.1　什么是欣赏型听力？

欣赏型听力，是指人们以愉悦或休闲为目的而进行的听力活动，如听音乐、看电影、听诗歌，等等。虽然这个概念目前还没有一个严格的定义，但是把它与前几章所讨论的理解型听力、思辨听力、跨文化听力和学术听力等区分开来并不难。从根本上说，欣赏歌曲或电影不同于在听力课堂里以获取信息、锻炼思辨、提高跨文化能力或者学术能力为目的的活动，它是以愉悦身心、休闲放松为目的。但是在教学实践中发现，当学生经常聆听外语歌曲或者观看外语影片的时候，确实有助于提高听说能力。逐渐地，听力课堂中也引入了欣赏型听力活动，并带有了教学目的。

即便如此，欣赏型听力活动还是具有与其他听力活动不同的特点。它以艺术欣赏和愉悦休闲为主要目的，因此任务压力较小，活动形式更为多样；相比常规的听力练习材料，歌曲或电影的语言鲜活、地道，内容更具艺术性、娱乐性和趣味性，对学生更具吸引力。欣赏型听力活动在课堂上的用途也逐渐变广。如果说早年的外语课堂上引入听歌和看电影是为了活跃课堂气氛或者介绍外国文化，那么现在外语教师运用欣赏型听力活动来促进教学的目标则更加丰富。精心设计的听歌或观剧活动，不仅能在课堂上用来训练微技能、开展跨文化思辨活动，还可以布置为课后的泛听练习。

6.2.2　欣赏型听力活动和语言学习的关系

首先，音乐和语言有密切的联系。心理学领域的研究发现，在大脑发展过程中，负责音乐和语言的区域是相互关联的。大脑能够理解音乐，并把音乐和语言中的节奏及句法，以相同的形式进行安排（McMullen & Saffran 2004）。研究还发现，音乐有助于语言学习。音乐刺激大脑，并帮助改善言语记忆和声音记忆。Wong 等（2007：420）认为，音乐和口头语言一样，都包含复杂的声音，都促进语言信息在脑干部分的编码。他们试图研究与音乐相关的体验是否能激活脑干中的编码，从而加强听觉功能，比如二语听力。于是，他们测试了音乐家和非音乐家对不同声调的反应，结果发现音乐家的大脑能更好地解码语言中的音高信息，因为这一过程与解码音乐中的声调有很多相近之处。因此，音乐能力能够帮助预测产生和感知二语中声音结构的能力。这一结论似乎有力地证明了二语学习者的音乐能力与语言能力的关系。

其次，Paivio（1986）的双码理论为电影教学在二语学习中的作用给出了理论依据（转引自沈渭菊 2011）。依据双码理论，人的记忆系统包括语言系统和非语言系统，当知识以语言系统与非语言系统共同编码时，比以单独的语言性系统或单独的非语言性系统进行编码，更容易被储存在记忆中。

6.2.3　欣赏型听力活动对听力教学的积极作用

1）激发学习兴趣，降低焦虑

听外语是最容易引发焦虑的学习活动之一。影响听力理解的因素很多，词汇量不足、注意力不集中、信息处理的效率不高、背景知识没有充分激活等都会导致听不懂。语言学习的焦虑感还与情境有关。听力课堂的教学方式如果是测试型的，也会使学生的焦虑感倍增。听歌和看电影这样的活动，恰好起到了缓和作用。曲调优美的外文经典歌曲，无疑能舒缓学生的紧张情绪。流畅的旋律，律动的节奏，充沛的情感，还能唤醒和激发学生的审美意识，而歌词本身也是诗性的语言，可用来欣赏。看外文电影、电视剧也是如此。被情节和人物吸引的同时，学习者已不知不觉沉浸在了语言中。平时担心自己词汇量不足或者跟不上正常语速的学生，在字幕的协助下，又有画面上人物动作、表情等帮助理解，完全可以欣赏影片。因此，听歌看剧，是激发学习者兴趣、降低焦虑的好办法。

2）提供原汁原味的语言输入

听外语歌曲和看外语影片另一个公认的优点，就是它们提供了原汁原味的语言输入。强调原声材料的重要性，体现了对语言实际运用能力的重视。听力课使用的材料中有相当一部分是专门为教材设计和录制的音视频。它们是在录音棚中专门制作，而不是来自生活中的真实语言片段。真实生活中的对话、新闻、广告、歌曲、影片、电视节目等则被称为原汁原味的材料。这样的语料包含了更多自然而鲜活的语言使用。

我们认为，教材编撰者采用专门制作的教学音视频，使其适合于学习者从低到高的语言水平发展，有其实用价值。这并不影响真实语料的使用。实际上，聆听真实语料是必不可少的。外语歌曲和影片就是学习者乐于接受的真实语料。看外语电影能让学习者犹如置身交际场景之中，听到真实交流中的语音语调，接触不同口音，听到语句的地道表达，有利于学习者掌握外语的实际运用能力。经常听歌，能训练学生感知韵律，体会语句中的押韵和节奏，辨别词汇间的连读。经常听歌，熟悉了歌词，还能学习词汇及用法，甚至学到歌词中的修辞手法。Warschauer 等（2000）曾经说过，语言学习最成功的时候是当它发生在真实而有意义的情境中的时候。我们听歌或看剧，往往就是以欣赏和娱乐的形式展开的对外语的真实使用。

3）增大输入的总量和频次

一部影片的时间往往长达一个小时以上，因此，看外语影片意味着学习者沉浸在所学语言中的时间比较长，语言输入量增加。听外语歌曲也是如此，因为喜爱，人们往往反复聆听，无形中提高了语言输入的频次，增加了语言输入的量。输入量和输入频次对语言习得有至关重要的作用，口头语言输入的总量和频次则直接影响听力能力。不达到一个基本的门槛，听力理解的熟练程度是不可能提高的。课堂上无法保证的训练量，需要课后补充。听歌和观剧以欣赏和娱乐为目的，压力小，心情放松，能保证课后的大量和多次输入。

4）呈现外国社会与文化

听歌曲和看影片等活动，能以更加生动的方式促进学习者对目的语国家社会和文化的了解。歌曲是社会实践的产物，能折射这个社会的哲学、政治、社会文化规则等多个方面（Kong 1995）。听经典歌曲时，除了欣赏韵律和美感，还可从歌曲背后的故事，窥见其创作时代的风貌。影片则承载了更多的信息，能生动再现历史上某个时代、事件或人物的片段或瞬间。例如，《莫扎特》《泰坦尼克号》《辛德勒的名单》等经典影片，在带给听力学习者艺术享受的同时，也丰富了他们对社会、历史和文化知识的了解。这些知识也成为学习者今后理解语言时不可缺少的背景知识储备。

6.3　欣赏型听力活动的教学目标

怎样利用欣赏型听力活动促进听力能力？我们发现，教师和学生对如何使用这类听力活动并不十分清楚。例如，该使用这种活动达到什么教学目的？该如何选择材料？是否能看字幕？应采用哪种语言的字幕？怎样设计任务？等等。我们认为，应重视并利用好这种类型的活动，在欣赏的同时促进语言学习和文化品鉴。需要说明的是，艺术欣赏力确实也是一种重要的能力，但不是本书的论述重点。本书关注的是欣赏型听力活动对语言习得和语言教学的促进作用。接下来以歌曲和影片为例，探讨欣赏型听力活动教学目标的设计。

6.3.1　活跃课堂气氛，寓教于乐

　　长时间、高强度的课堂听力训练难免令人疲倦，导致学习效率下降，而合适的歌曲和影视片段几乎总是可以给课堂带来轻松活泼的氛围，让紧绷的神经得到舒缓。王红（2000）较早就展开了对"听歌法"的研究，发现 75% 的大学英语学习者喜欢以赏析经典英文歌曲作为学习内容。她在教学中的做法是精选一首优美的歌曲在主导的教学任务结束后播放，使学生的身心得到放松，再过渡到下一教学内容中。王秋云（2015）则认为，用英文歌曲开始一堂课，可以使学生的情绪轻松愉悦，增加学习兴趣和动力，还能拉近师生之间的关系。因此，教师应善于利用歌曲或影视剧的有趣片段，调节课堂氛围，增加学习乐趣。

6.3.2　提供真实语言场景，训练听力基本功

　　歌曲和影片本身就是训练语言基本功的绝佳素材。听外语歌曲可以体会歌词的韵律，同样也可以练习识别连读、缩略、同化等词汇边界的发音现象；反复聆听一首优美的歌曲并模仿、吟唱，还可以改善学生的外语发音。因此，教师用歌曲来讲解辨音和发音规则，语料真实，比一般的例句更令人印象深刻。歌曲还可以用来给初级水平的学生做句子节奏训练（满蓉、王劲 2011）。

　　视频相对于音频的优势在于画面。影视片段提供的真实语言场景，能弥补书本的不足。Holland & Adamson（2017）发现，用电影让学生学语言，最能吸引学生，也最能让他们产生共鸣。他们认为，电影就像一个取之不尽用之不竭的宝库，可以用来实现几乎所有的听力技能训练，还能帮助提高学生的跨文化能力、语用能力以及提升他们的外语流利度、准确度，甚至可以作为足不出户的"实地考察"。影片带给我们的真实感，来自于画面和情节所展示的情境。观察真实交流中的动作、手势、眼神等副语言信息，分析真实交流发生的时间、地点和环境等，都有助于理解语言。此时，影片很好地弥补了音频材料的不足。因此，提供语言运用的真实场景，是欣赏型活动的另一个教学目标。

6.3.3 确保听力输入的量

没有足够量的练习，听力就无法达到熟练程度。所以，几乎每个听力教师都会建议学生多听。课堂时间有限，而且大多数是"精听"，即对语音、词汇、语法、句子意思等的理解做准确精细的教学要求。而"泛听"的任务多布置在课后，主要用来保证口头语言的大量输入。研究发现，"泛听"对听力理解能力有明显的促进作用（Chang 2010；Chang & Millett 2014）。然而，大多数学习者并不能做好"泛听"，其中一个主要原因就是不能坚持。与听新闻、做听写、刷听力题目等练习相比，听歌追剧要容易坚持得多。其欣赏或娱乐的目的，无意中造就了对外语的长时间输入和反复输入。因此，布置欣赏型活动作为泛听任务，是一个很好的选择。

6.3.4 增加生词的附带习得

欣赏型听力活动的另一个重要目标，是扩大听力词汇的附带习得。在欣赏型活动中，听者的目的并不是有意识地去学习，但是无意中长时间、多次地听一些词汇，不但会牢固地记住它们的发音，还能从语境中猜出词义。这就形成了附带习得。电影字幕的使用，也可促进附带习得的产生。字幕的英文是subtitles 或 captions，前者指被翻译成听者本国语言的字幕，后者是指仍旧是外国语言的字幕（Markham 1999）。对英文影片来说，就是分别指中文字幕和英文字幕。Vanderplank（1994，2010）认为，纪录片或情景喜剧的字幕能为学习者提供丰富的语言资源；字幕在训练学生听力技能和识别所听词汇方面有很大价值，在字幕中见过的词，以后再出现，更容易识别。同时他也建议，要想发挥字幕的有益作用，必须在字幕质量、视频材料本身难度（根据学生语言水平判断）、学生的阅读技能和听力技能之间做好平衡。

6.3.5 提高跨文化能力

欣赏型听力活动可用来提高跨文化能力。本书第四章已详细叙述跨文化能力的教学目标：识别、阐释、对比和评价听力材料中的文化现象。欣赏型活动，特别是观看影片，可布置为课后活动，用来作为课堂跨文化能力训练的延伸。

6.4　欣赏型听力教学设计实例

这一部分将以听歌和看影片为例，针对上述教学目标分别设计教学活动。每个教学活动包括要点讲解、课前准备、活动实例、音视频文本、变化与拓展。

6.4.1　欣赏型听力活动设计一：纠正发音、掌握节奏

1）要点讲解

听歌促进听力学习的独特作用，在于听者因喜爱而反复聆听，从而将语言和音律融合在一起而产生深刻记忆。说话时，单词和句子的发音规律在歌唱时往往依然存在，但是歌唱中的吐字更清晰，能使听者更清楚地辨别发音、感知词汇边界的音变现象，还能体会节奏和韵律。反复聆听后产生的记忆使听者能够更准确地模仿词汇发音、掌握句子节奏。

学生是歌曲听众中的一个庞大群体，在他们经常聆听的流行歌曲中，英文歌曲占据不小的比例。听谁的歌、听什么歌，个人可根据自己的喜好随心挑选，但是教师用作欣赏型活动的歌曲却需要精心安排。首先要考虑学生的水平。对基础水平的学生，应选择吐词速度较慢、歌词难度较低的歌曲。其次，要考虑教学目标。有的歌曲适合学习辨音，有的歌曲适合学习某个语法现象（如虚拟），有的适合学习词汇。选择得好，即使是附带习得，效果也好。经典歌曲，经久不衰，比较适合选用为欣赏型听力活动的材料。

2）课前准备

（1）选择一首英文歌曲。教师准备好音频或者视频，将歌词准备成幻灯或者打印出来。

（2）将歌词里押头韵或尾韵的地方，或者有连读、同化的地方划上下划线，

根据教学目标制作填空题。

(3) 准备歌曲背景介绍、歌手介绍，制成问答题或趣味智力抢答题；对比较陌生的单词添加注释。

3）活动实例

听前

教师让学生先熟悉歌曲的时代背景，了解歌手的基本信息。这里以《寂静之声》为例。这是一首 19 世纪 60 年代的美国民谣，配乐上带有一些摇滚风格，因此这首歌也被认为是一首民谣摇滚 (Folk Rock)。演唱者为西蒙和加芬克尔 (Simon & Garfunkel) 组合。

听中

播放歌曲全曲或片段让学生们欣赏。解释活动的目的是练习语音流的切分。这里可以视情况补充一些知识点。听第二遍，一边听，一边完成填空练习。然后，将歌词投在屏幕上，或将打印歌词的纸条发给学生核对。

以下为练习示例（括号内为应填出的歌词）：

Hello darkness, _____, (my old friend)

_____ with you again, (I've come to talk)

Because a vision softly creeping,

_____while I was sleeping, (Left its seeds)

And the vision that _____ my brain (was planted in)

Still remains

Within the sound of silence.

_____ I walked alone (In restless dreams)

Narrow streets of cobblestone,

'Neath the halo of a street lamp,

I turned my collar to the _____. (cold and damp)

When my eyes _____the flash of a neon light (were stabbed by)

That split the night

And _____ the sound of silence. (touched)

听后

在核对完整的歌词后，教师逐一分析词汇边界的音变现象：在 my old friend 中，old 的 /d/ 音被同化了，听不到这个音；I've come to talk 中的 to 弱化了；Left its seeds 中，left 结尾的 /t/ 和 its 的词首元音 /i/ 形成连读；was planted in 中，planted 结尾的 /d/ 和 in 的词首元音 /i/ 形成连读；In restless dreams 中，restless 一词中的 /t/ 几乎没有发音，这是词中的同化现象；cold and damp 中，cold 中的 /d/ 和 and 的词首元音 /ə/ 连读，and 词尾的 /d/ 和 damp 的第一个辅音 /d/ 合二为一，也就是 and 的头尾都与其相邻的边界发生了连读；were stabbed by 中的 stabbed 本应有一个尾音 /d/，但是被同化，没有发出来；touched 最后一个音 /t/ 也几乎没有，属于同化现象。教师提醒学生在说英语时同样要注意词汇连接处的发音。

4）音视频文本

The Sound of Silence

Hello darkness, my old friend,

I've come to talk with you again,

Because a vision softly creeping,

Left its seeds while I was sleeping,

And the vision that was planted in my brain

Still remains

Within the sound of silence.

In restless dreams I walked alone

Narrow streets of cobblestone.

'Neath the halo of a street lamp,

I turned my collar to the cold and damp

When my eyes were stabbed by the flash of a neon light

That split the night

And touched the sound of silence.

And in the naked light I saw

Ten thousand people, maybe more.

People talking without speaking,

People hearing without listening,

People writing songs that voices never share

And no one dared

Disturb the sound of silence.

"Fools," said I. "You do not know.

Silence like a cancer grows.

Hear my words that I might teach you.

Take my arms that I might reach you."

But my words like silent raindrops fell

And echoed in the wells of silence.

And the people bowed and prayed

To the neon God they made.

And the sign flashed out its warning

In the words that it was forming.

And the sign said, "The words of the prophets are written on the subway walls

And tenement halls

And whispered in the sounds of silence."

5）变化与拓展

听歌练习的另一种常见形式，是体会歌词的押韵。还是以《寂静之声》为例，可设计练习如下：

Hello darkness, my old _____,

I've come to talk with you _____,

Because a vision softly _____,

Left its seeds while I was _____,

And the vision that was planted in my _____

Still _____

Within the sound of silence.

In restless dreams I walked _____

Narrow streets of _____.

'Neath the halo of a street _____,

I turned my collar to the cold and _____

When my eyes were stabbed by the flash of a neon _____

That split the _____

And touched the sound of silence.

这里押韵的词分别是 friend 和 again，creeping 和 sleeping，brain 和 remain(s)，alone 和 cobblestone，lamp 和 damp，light 和 night。

教学上一般倾向于挑选曲调简洁优美、节奏平稳、吐字清晰、朗朗上口，有一定流行度的歌曲，这些歌曲在民谣类和流行歌曲类的作品中比较容易找到。也可请每位学生推荐一首自己喜欢的歌曲，这样形成一份内容丰富、风格多样的歌单，分享给大家课后聆听。

6.4.2 欣赏型听力活动设计二：增加词汇的附带习得

1）要点讲解

附带习得是二语学习者词汇发展的主要方式（Webb & Nation 2017）。在前面几章提到的听力词汇量缺口，实际上也要靠附带习得来补上。研究表明，看外语影片和短视频都能产生明显的附带习得（Peters & Webb 2018；Rodgers & Webb 2020）。也就是说，在欣赏外语影片的同时，还能够增加词汇量。这里说的词汇量，不仅包括单词，还包括常用的词组、地道的俗语，等等。看整部影片或者电视连续剧，都只适合课外进行。但是，教师在课堂上可以采用电影片段，把促进附带习得的方法教给学生。

例如，怎样利用好字幕？在 20 世纪 80 年代，在录像制品上打出字幕最初是为有听力障碍的人所用，但是来自哈佛大学英语作为第二语言研究与发展中心的 Price（1983）首先关注到字幕对于语言学习者的影响。她通过对 500 名具有 20 种不同母语背景和不同教育水平的学生的实验研究发现，看带有字幕的视频有助于语言的理解和习得。之后，不少研究证实了她的发现。但是，也有人（如 Vandergrift & Cross 2014；Vanderplank 1990）提出一些问题，如边看电影边看字幕，是否会分散观影者的注意？注意力是集中在画面上还是语言上？阅读水平是否会从中起到影响？母语不使用罗马字母（如中文、阿拉伯语）的学生与母语使用罗马字母（如法语、德语）的学生看字幕的效果是否一样？这些问题还有待进一步研究。但是可以肯定的是，字幕应根据学生的情况合理运用。如果内容不难，没有很多生僻的词汇，可以尝试第一遍不用字幕。在观看第二遍或第三遍后再打开字幕，看看难点在哪里。如果需要打开字幕，也应首选外语字幕而不是翻译成母语的字幕。这是因为，大脑里已经留下较深印象的生词发音和意思，再与词汇的拼写形式合在一起，更易于记忆。这种方法还有助于学生将只看得懂或者只听得懂的词进行更为全面地学习。

2）课前准备

故事片大多以场景、画面、情节和对话来展现剧情发展，而纪录片除了靠丰富的画面，还要依靠解说词来传达主旨。这样的解说词信息量大、词汇丰富、结构清晰、逻辑严密，适合用在以增加词汇量为附带习得目的的欣赏型听力活动中。本例选用的是介绍宇宙起源的科普纪录片，知识性强，主题非常鲜明，适合用来附带习得这一类词汇。需提前准备相关词汇的中英文释义，以及听前热身练习用的问题。例如：

- How old is our universe?
- Where does it come from?
- Do you know any theory of the formation of the universe?

3）活动实例

听前

本纪录片系列有几十集，课堂上选用第一集的片段，时长 2 分钟。看影片之前，询问同学是否知道宇宙的起源。可让学生与同伴或与前后桌组成小组，讨论后回答。

听中

观看影片，第一遍不显示字幕，在观看第二遍时开启字幕。看完两遍之后，请学生简要介绍此片段的大意。全程并不进行单词学习，但是在讨论和回答问题时，如果学生询问到生词，可以给予中英文释义。活动的焦点在于通过观赏影片，了解宇宙的起源。

听后

教师对所听内容做一个简单的回顾，刻意使用材料里含有的但是学生不熟悉的词。之后，教师提出一个发散性的问题：

Is the Big Bang a theory or a fact? State your reasons.

学生在表达自己观点时，再次使用到附带习得的词汇。对意见不一致的地方，教师建议学生们回去查找资料。对剩余片段的观看，教师布置为家庭作业，同时也应布置讨论题和写作任务。

4）音视频文本

Voiceover：Our universe is now 380,000 years old, and trillions and trillions of miles across. Clouds of hydrogen and helium gas float through space. It will take another 200 million years before those gasses create the first stars.

Interviewee 1：The first stars ignited the universe into what must have been the most amazing fireworks. The universe went from the Dark Ages to an age of splendor when the first stars illuminated the gas and the universe began to glow in majestic fashion. I wish I'd been there.

Interviewee 2：It was like Christmas tree lights turning on. The universe began to light up in all directions until you form the beautiful mosaic we now see today.

Voiceover：More and more stars turn on. One billion years after the Big Bang, the first galaxy forms. Over the next eight billion years, countless more take shape. Then, about five billion years ago, in a quiet corner of one of those galaxies, gravity begins to draw in dust and gas. Gradually, they clump together and give birth to a star: our sun. Nine billion years after the Big Bang, our tiny solar system springs to life, and with it, planet Earth. Everything there exists because of the Big Bang and it's still going on. Our universe is still expanding, but it won't just keep going forever. Our universe had a beginning and it will also have an end.

（选自纪录片 *How the Universe Works*）

5）变化与拓展

当学生学业繁忙，课后也没有大量时间去观影追剧的时候，教师可以向他们推荐 20 分钟左右的影视片段。这些片段中最好有一些高频次出现的生词，这样的生词被习得的概率更高。教师可注意积累这样的片段。不论是纪录片还是故事片，都可以作为来源。

6.4.3　欣赏型听力活动设计三：学配音，观察副语言

1）要点讲解

模仿，是口语学习的常用策略。初学者常常通过模仿使自己的语音语调更加自然和地道。在 20 世纪 80 年代，我国的英语学习者通过听磁带来模仿《英语九百句》《新概念英语》，而现在流行的是使用智能手机软件给电影人物配音，更加方便、有趣。配音要求准确模仿语音、语调，并且在节奏、语速、音色、吐字上尽量靠近原角色。要想做到这一点，不仅需要准确地感知和辨别，还需要多次聆听，才能模仿到位。因此，这一口语活动同时也能训练听力。

这里不得不提到副语言。副语言包括说话的语气、速度、音量、流利程度等。也有人把副语言的范围扩大到说话时的动作、表情、姿势、手势，等等。听辨和观察这些伴随着语言而发生的非语言交流特征，能够有效地促进听力理解。这也是看电影学外语的一个优势。配音活动可以锻炼这种非语言交流能力。

2）课前准备

准备含有丰富对白的电影片段，根据剧情分析人物心理，分析对白中的语言和非语言特征。对白的脚本也要提前准备好。

3）活动实例

听前

观影前，教师先介绍本次活动的目的：学配音，观察副语言。教师介绍什么是副语言，并以改变自己的声调、语速、表情、姿势等作为例子来讲解。然后，介绍该片段之前的剧情。本例选择的片段来自影片《当幸福来敲门》(*The Pursuit of Happiness*)。影片的主角 Chris Gardner 靠推销产品艰辛度日，他想报考证券公司的经纪人职位来改变生活。这个职位需要培训，而能否参加培训还需要面试。在面试的前一天，他正在粉刷墙壁，却不承想因无钱支付停车费，

155

被警察找上门，结果在警察局蹲了一晚。第二天，他狂奔去证券公司，穿着满是白漆的脏外套出现在面试官面前。他该如何通过这场重要的面试呢？

听中

Mr. Twistle 是证券公司的经理，因曾与 Chris 有一面之缘，知道他天资聪颖，是个很好的候选人。但是，当他看到 Chris 一身邋遢，不禁面露尴尬。总裁 Mr. Frohm 虽然没有以貌取人，但是也没有绕过衣着不得体的问题。Chris 紧张而又力图表现自信，他用幽默化解了眼前的尴尬。这一片段在影片中非常关键，情节紧凑、很吸引人。教师让学生先仔细聆听人物说话时的语气、节奏和语调，观察演员的眼神、表情、手势和动作，然后模仿这一片段进行配音。

听后

教师点评学生的表现，学生之间也可以互评。教师总结副语言在人际交流中不可或缺的作用。布置电影、电视剧片段配音的家庭作业。

4）音视频文本

Chris: Chris Gardner. How are you? Good morning! (To Mr. Frohm) Chris Gardner. (To Mr. Twistle) Chris Gardner. Good to see you again. (To another interviewer) Chris Gardner. Pleasure. I've been sitting there for the last half hour trying to come up with a story that would explain my being here dressed like this. And…And I wanted to come up with a story that would demonstrate qualities that I am sure you all admire here, like earnestness or diligence, and team-playing, something. And I couldn't think…of anything. So, the truth is I was arrested for failure to pay parking tickets.

Mr. Twistle: Parking tickets? What?

Chris: And I ran all the way here from the…The Polk Station, the police station.

Mr. Frohm: What were you doing before you were arrested?

Chris: I was, uh…painting my apartment.

Mr. Frohm: Is it dry now?

Chris: Uh, I hope so.

Mr. Frohm: Jay says you're pretty determined.

Mr. Twistle: Oh, he's been waiting outside the front of the building with some 40-pound gizmo for over a month.

Mr. Frohm: He said you're smart.

Chris: Well, I like to think so.

Mr. Frohm: And you want to learn this business?

Chris: Yes, sir. I wanna learn this business.

Mr. Frohm: Have you already started learning on your own?

Chris: Absolutely.

Mr. Frohm: Jay?

Mr. Twistle: Yes, sir.

Mr. Frohm: How many times have you seen Chris?

Mr. Twistle: Yeah, I don't know. One too many, apparently.

Mr. Frohm: Was he ever dressed like this?

Mr. Twistle: No, no. Jacket and tie.

Mr. Frohm: First in your class in school? High school?

Chris: Yes, sir.

Mr. Frohm: How many in the class?

Chris: Uh, 12. It was a small town.

Mr. Frohm: I'll say.

Chris: But I was also first in my radar class in the Navy, and that was a class of 20. Can I say something? Um…Um…I'm the type of person, if you ask me a question, and I don't know the answer, I'm gonna tell you that I don't know. But I bet you what. I know how to find the answer. Is that fair enough?

Mr. Frohm: Chris, what would you say if a guy walked in for an interview without a shirt on and I hire him? What would you say?

Chris: He must've had on some really nice pants.

(They all laugh.)

5）变化与拓展

角色扮演或戏剧表演，可作为一种拓展形式用于学习副语言。如果说配音主要看语言上的表现，那么表演就还要配合表情、动作、姿态等多个方面。这种活动以其生动和有趣，一直受到外语学习者的喜爱。

6.4.4 欣赏型听力活动设计四：跨文化对比

1）要点讲解

使用影片做跨文化对比，具有事半功倍的效果。文化在生活中无处不在，而影片是生活的写照。仔细观看外语影片，从中不难发现影片中国家的风土人情、社会百态。更有一些影片，正是以文化对比为主题。运用好这一宝贵资源，可以把跨文化听力活动安排得有声有色。跨文化听力教学在第四章有详细论述，这里不再赘述。

2）课前准备

影片《我盛大的希腊婚礼》（*My Big Fat Greek Wedding*）从头至尾都充满希腊文化和美国文化的对比，而影片《涉外大饭店》（*The Best Exotic Marigold Hotel*）则是将西方文化和东方文化进行对比。两部电影都是轻喜剧，难度适中，适合学习者观看。

3）活动实例

听前

整部影片布置给学生在课后观看，课堂上播放的是影片开头 5 分钟，用来介绍跨文化对比的任务。听前，根据影片的背景，在班级展开对子或小组讨论。讨论题示例为：美国是一个移民国家，在美国的少数族裔如何保持自己的传统？他们的下一代会如何看待祖辈的传统？

听中

教师放映影片开头的这个片段。清晨 5 点，天还没有亮。在滂沱大雨中，芝加哥一家希腊餐厅 Dancing Zorba's 的老板和他的女儿就已经出发去店里上班了。车里，慈爱的老父亲看着老大不小还未出嫁的女儿 Toula，叹了一口气说："You better get married soon. You are starting to look old." 女儿无奈地看了一眼老爸，她的独白画外音传来。影片就这样开始。

影片中，以父亲为代表的老一代希腊人，尽管移民到美国，但还是保持着希腊民族传统的家庭观、婚姻观和生活方式。然而，他的在美国长大的女儿 Toula 却不想那么"传统"：她想做一份自己喜欢的工作，而不是在家族餐馆里打工。她爱上教师 Ian，却发现两人除了种族不同，宗教信仰不同，家庭也很不一样。来自不同文化背景的两个人是否能走到一起？

看完片段后，教师邀请 1—2 名同学，对影片的内容做出推测。

听后

教师布置作业：课后观看整部影片，注意影片中文化细节的对比，归纳出希腊文化与美国文化的代表性特征，思考它们与中国文化的异同，并设想若自己身处多元文化的情境下，应怎样与人交往。任务布置为四人小组合作完成，下一周在课堂以小组形式做展示，分享观点。

4）音视频文本

Father:　　　You better get married soon. You are starting to look old.

Voiceover:　　My dad has been saying that to me since I was 15, because nice Greek

　　　　　　　girls are supposed to do three things in life: Marry Greek boys, make

Greek babies and feed everyone...until the day we die. When I was growing up, I knew I was different. The other girls were blond and delicate, and I was a swarthy 6-year-old with sideburns. I so badly wanted to be like the popular girls all sitting together, talking...eating their wonder Bread sandwiches.

A young girl: What's that? It's moussaka (一种肉和茄子做成的希腊菜).

Young Toula: Moose ka-ka?

Voiceover: And while the pretty girls got to go to Brownies (幼年女童子军), I had to go to Greek school. At Greek school, I learned valuable lessons like: "If Nick has one goat and Maria has nine, how soon will they marry?" My mom was always cooking foods filled with warmth and wisdom and never forgetting that side dish of steaming-hot guilt.

Mother: Niko, don't play with your food. When I was your age, we didn't even have food.

Young Toula: Ma?

Mother: What?

Young Toula: Why do I have to go to Greek school?

Mother: When you get married, don't you want to be able to write your mother-in-law a letter? Niko, come on, eat!

Voiceover: We lived in a normal, middle-class Chicago neighborhood of tasteful, modest homes. Our house, however, was modeled after the Parthenon (帕特农神庙), complete with Corinthian columns, and guarded by statues of the gods. In case the neighbors had any doubts about our heritage, they could just check out our subtle tribute to the great flag. My dad believed in only two things, that Greeks should educate non-Greeks about being Greek, and that any ailment, from psoriasis to poison ivy, could be cured with Windex.

5）变化与拓展

可用来做跨文化对比的影片或电视剧还是较多的，有的是整部剧都可用，有的则是部分片段可用。除了中外文化对比外，还可进行外国文化之间的对比。在活动形式上，还可采用不同小组观看不同影片的方式。这样，在班级上进行小组分享时，内容就会更丰富，视野更开阔。

参考文献

Abedi, J. & C. Lord. 2001. The language factor in mathematics tests. *Applied Measurement in Education* 14(3): 219-234.

ACTFL. 1996. *Standards for Foreign Language Learning: Preparing for the 21st Century.* Lawrence, KS: Allen Press.

Al-jasser, F. 2008. The effect of teaching English phonotactics on the lexical segmentation of English as a foreign language. *System* 36(1): 94-106.

Anderson, J. R. 2000. *Cognitive Psychology and Its Implications* (5th ed.). New York: Worth Publishing.

Anderson, L. W. & D. R. Krathwohl. 2001. *A Taxonomy for Learning, Teaching and Assessing: A Revision of Bloom's Taxonomy of Educational Objectives* (Complete Edition). New York: Longman.

Arnold, J. 2000. Seeing through listening comprehension exam anxiety. *TESOL Quarterly* 34(4): 777-786.

Aryadoust, V. 2018. Taxonomies of listening skills. In J. I. Liontas (ed.). *The TESOL Encyclopedia of English Language Teaching* (1st ed.). Hoboken, NJ: John Wiley & Sons. 1-8.

Bacon, S. M. 1992. The relationship between gender, comprehension, processing strategies, and cognitive and affective response in foreign language listening. *The Modern Language Journal* 76(2): 160-178.

Baddeley, A. D. & G. Hitch. 1974. Working memory. In G. A. Bower (ed.). *The Psychology of Learning and Motivation* (vol. 8). New York: Academic Press. 47-89

Beall, M. L. 2010. Perspectives on intercultural listening. In A. D. Wolvin (ed.). *Listening and Human Communication in the 21st Century.* Oxford: Wiley-Blackwell. 225-238.

Beebe, S. A. & S. J. Beebe. 2009. *A Concise Public Speaking Handbook* (2nd ed.). Boston: Pearson Education.

Bloom, B., M. Englehart, E. Furst, W. Hill & D. Krathwohl. 1956. *Taxonomy of Educational Objectives: The Classification of Educational Goals. Handbook I: Cognitive Domain.* New York/Toronto: Longmans, Green.

Bonk, W. J. 2000. Second language lexical knowledge and listening comprehension.

International Journal of Listening 14(1): 14-31.

Boyle, J. P. 1984. Factors affecting listening comprehension. *ELT Journal* 38(1): 34-38.

Brown, G. 1995. *Speakers, Listeners and Communication: Explorations in Discourse Analysis*. Cambridge: Cambridge University Press.

Brown, J. D. 2012. *New Ways in Teaching Connected Speech*. Alexandria: TESOL International Association.

Brown, R., R. Waring & S. Donkaewbua. 2008. Incidental vocabulary acquisition from reading, reading-while-listening, and listening to stories. *Reading in a Foreign Language* 20(2):136-163.

Brownell, J. 2010. The skills of listening-centered communication. In A. D. Wolvin (ed.). *Listening and Human Communication in the 21st Century.* Oxford: Wiley-Blackwell. 141-157.

Buck, G. 1995. How to become a good listening teacher. In D. Mendelsohn & J. Rubin (eds.). *A Guide for the Teaching of Second Language Listening.* San Diego: Dominie Press. 113-131.

Buck, G. 2001. *Assessing Listening.* Cambridge: Cambridge University Press.

Byram, M. 1997. *Teaching and Assessing Intercultural Communicative Competence.* Clevedon: Multilingual Matters.

Canale, M. & M. Swain. 1980. Theoretical bases of communicative approaches to second language teaching and testing. *Applied Linguistics* 1(1): 1-47.

Carrell, P. L., P. A. Dunkel & P. Molluan. 2002. *The Effects of Notetaking, Lecture Length and Topic on the Listening Component of the TOEFL 2000.* (TOEFL Monograph Series No. MS-23). Princeton: Educational Testing Service.

Chamot, A. U. & J. M. O' Malley. 1994. *The CALLA Handbook: Implementing the Cognitive Academic Language Learning Approach.* White Plain: Addison Wesley Longman.

Chan, R. Y. P. 1995. Language in lecturing: A study of discourse markers in computer science and information systems lectures [Unpublished master's thesis]. Hong Kong: City University of Hong Kong.

Chang, A. C-S. 2010. Second-language listening anxiety before and after a 1-yr. intervention in extensive listening compared with standard foreign language instruction. *Perceptual and Motor Skills* 110(2): 355-365.

Chang, A. C-S. & S. Millett. 2014. The effect of extensive listening on developing L2 listening fluency: Some hard evidence. *ELT Journal* 68(1): 31-40.

Chaudron, C., L. Loschky & J. Cook. 1994. Second language listening comprehension and lecture note-taking. In J. Flowerdew (ed.). *Academic Listening Research Perspectives*. Cambridge: Cambridge University Press. 75-92.

Chen, G. M. 2010. *Foundations of Intercultural Communication Competence*. Hong Kong: China Review Academic Publishers.

Chiang, C. S. & P. Dunkel. 1992. The effect of speech modification, prior knowledge and listening proficiency on EFL lecture learning. *TESOL Quarterly* 26(2): 345-369.

Clark, M., S. Wayland, S. Castle & K. Gynther. 2013. The effects of note-taking on L2 listening comprehension: Assessment plan (TTO 2012 Technical Report 2.1). College Park: University of Maryland Center for Advanced Study of Language.

Clinard, H. 1985. Listen for the difference. *Training and Development Journal* (39): 10-39.

Cross, J. 2010. Raising L2 listeners' metacognitive awareness: A sociocultural theory perspective. *Language Awareness* 19(4): 281-297.

Cutler, A. 1997. The comparative perspective on spoken language processing. *Speech Communication* 21(1-2): 3-15.

Dang, T. N. Y. & S. Webb. 2014. The lexical profile of academic spoken English. *English for Specific Purposes* 33: 66-76.

Deardorff, D. K. 2006. The identification and assessment of intercultural competence as a student outcome of internationalization at institutions of higher education in the United States. *Journal of Studies in International Education* 10(3): 241-266.

Deardorff, D. K. 2011. Assessing intercultural competence. *New Directions for Institutional Research* 149: 65-79.

Dejean de la Batie, B. & D. C. Bradley. 1995. Resolving word boundaries in spoken French: Native and non-native strategies. *Applied Psycholinguistics* 16(1): 59-81.

Dudley-Evans, T. 1994. Genre analysis: An approach to text analysis for ESP. In M. Coulthard (ed.). *Advances in Written Text Analysis*. London: Routledge. 219-228.

Duker, S. 1962. Basics in critical listening. *The English Journal* 51(8): 565-567.

Dunkel, P. 1991. Listening in the native and second/foreign language: Toward an integration of research and practice. *TESOL Quarterly* 25(3): 431-457.

Dwyer, C. P., M. J. Hogan & I. Stewart. 2014. An integrated critical thinking framework for the 21st century. *Thinking Skills & Creativity* 12: 43-52.

Facione, P. A. 1990. *Critical Thinking: A Statement of Expert Consensus for Purposes of Educational Assessment and Instruction – The Delphi Report*. Millbrae: California Academic Press.

Faerch, C. & G. Kasper. 1986. One learner two languages: Investigating types of interlanguage knowledge. In J. House & S. Blum-Kulka (eds.). *Interlingual and Intercultural Communication: Discourse and Cognition in Translation and Second Language Acquisition Studies*. Tuebingen: Gunter Narr. 211-227.

Fantini, A. E. 2009. Assessing intercultural competence: Issues and tools. In D. K. Deardorff, (ed.). *The SAGE Handbook of Intercultural Competence*. Thousand Oaks: SAGE. 456-476.

Field, J. 2003. Promoting perception: Lexical segmentation in L2 listening. *ELT Journal* 57(4): 325-334.

Field, J. 2008. *Listening in the Language Classroom*. Cambridge: Cambridge University Press.

Flowerdew, J. & L. Miller. 1997. The teaching of academic listening comprehension and the question of authenticity. *English for Specific Purposes Journal* 16(1): 27-46.

Flowerdew, J. & L. Miller. 2005. *Second Language Listening: Theory and Practice*. New York: Cambridge University Press.

Gass, S. M. & A. Mackey. 2015. Input, interaction, and output in second language acquisition. In B. VanPatten & J. Williams (eds.). *Theories in Second Language Acquisition* (2nd ed.). New York: Routledge. 180-206.

Gass, S. M., A. Mackey & L. Ross-Feldman. 2005. Task-based interactions in classroom and laboratory settings. *Language Learning* 55(4): 575-611.

Gathercole, S. E. & A. D. Baddeley. 1993. *Working Memory and Language*. Hillside: Lawrence Erlbaum Associates.

Goh, C. C. M. 2013. ESP and listening. In B. Paltridge & S. Starfield (eds.). *The Handbook of English for Specific Purposes*. Hoboken, NJ: John Wiley & Sons. 55-76.

Goh, C. C. M. & V. Aryadoust. 2015. Examining the notion of listening subskill divisibility and its implications for second language listening. *International Journal of Listening* 29(3): 109-133.

Graham, S. & E. Macaro. 2008. Strategy instruction in listening for lower-intermediate learners of French. *Language Learning* 58(4): 747-783.

Heller, V. & M. Morek. 2015. Academic discourse as situated practice: An introduction. *Linguistics and Education* 31: 174-186.

Holland, L. & T. Adamson. 2017. Whole movies and clips to promote focused listening. *The ORTESOL Journal* 34: 53-76.

Hood, S. & G. Forey. 2005. Introducing a conference paper: Getting interpersonal with your audience. *Journal of English for Academic Purposes* 4(4): 291-306.

Hu, M., & I. S. P. Nation. 2000. Unknown vocabulary density and reading comprehension. *Reading in a Foreign Language* 13(1): 403-430.

Jacquemot, C. & S. K. Scott. 2006. What is the relationship between phonological short-term memory and speech processing? *Trends in Cognitive Science* 10(11): 480-486.

Jordan, R. R. 1997. *English for Academic Purposes: A Guide and Resources Book for Teachers.* Cambridge: Cambridge University Press.

Jung, E. H. 2003. The role of discourse signaling cues in second language listening comprehension. *The Modern Language Journal* 87(4): 562-577.

Kelly, P. 1991. Lexical ignorance: The main obstacle to listening comprehension with advanced foreign language learners. *International Review of Applied Linguistics in Language Teaching* 29(2): 135-149.

Kong, L. 1995. Music and cultural politics: Ideology and resistance in Singapore. *Transactions of the Institute of British Geographers* 20(4): 447-459.

Laufer, B. & G. C. Ravenhorst-Kalovski. 2010. Lexical threshold revisited: Lexical text coverage, learners' vocabulary size and reading comprehension. *Reading in a Foreign Language* 22(1): 15-30.

Lin, M. 2006. The effects of note-taking, memory and rate of presentation on EFL learners' listening comprehension. [Unpublished PhD Dissertation]. California: La Sierra University.

Littlemore, J. 2001. The use of metaphor in university lectures and the problems that it causes for overseas students. *Teaching in Higher Education* 6(3): 333-349.

Liu, N. F. 2003. Processing problems in L2 listening comprehension of university students in Hong Kong. [PhD Dissertation]. Hong Kong: Hong Kong Polytechnic University.

Loewen, S. 2005. Incidental focus on form and second language learning. *Studies in Second Language Acquisition* 27(3): 361-386.

Long, M. H. 1996. The role of the linguistic environment in second language acquisition. In W. C. Ritchie & T. K. Bhatia (eds.). *Handbook of Second Language Acquisition* (vol. 2). New York: Academic Press. 413-468.

Lucas, S. E. 2008. *The Art of Public Speaking* (10th ed.). New York: McGraw Hill.

Lundsteen, S. W. 1966. Critical listening: An experiment. *The Elementary School Journal* 66(6): 311-315.

Lustig, M. W. & J. Koester. 2006. *Intercultural Competence: Interpersonal Communication Across Cultures* (5th ed.). Boston: Pearson Education.

Lynch, T. 2011. Academic listening in the 21st century: Reviewing a decade of research. *Journal of English for Academic Purposes* 10(2): 79-88.

Markham, P. 1999. Captioned videotapes and second language listening word recognition. *Foreign Language Annals* 32(3): 321-328.

Martin, J. N. & T. K. Nakayama. 2004. *Intercultural Communication in Contexts* (3rd ed.). New York: McGraw Hill.

Marx, A., B. Heppt & S. Henschel. 2016. Listening comprehension of academic and everyday language in first language and second language students. *Applied Psycholinguistics* 38(3): 571-600.

McClelland, J. L. & D. E. Rumelhart. 1981. An interactive activation model of context effects in letter perception: Part 1. An account of basic findings. *Psychological Review* 88(5): 375-407.

McKinnon, S. 2013. What is intercultural competence? Global Perspectives Project. http://www.gcu.ac.uk/media/gcalwebv2/theuniversity/centresprojects/globalperspectives/Definition_of_Intercultural_competence.pdf (accessed 12/03/2018).

McMullen, E. & J. R. Saffran. 2004. Music and language: A developmental comparison. *Music Perception* 21(3): 289-311.

Mecartty, F. 2000. Lexical and grammatical knowledge in reading and listening comprehension by foreign language learners of Spanish. *Applied Language Learning* 11(2): 323-348.

Mendelsohn, D. 1995. Applying learning strategies in the second/foreign language listening comprehension lesson. In D. Mendelsohn & J. Rubin (eds.). *A Guide for the Teaching of Second Language Listening.* San Diego: Dominie Press. 132-150.

Monrad-Krohn, G. H. 1947. Dysprosody or altered melody of language. *Brain* 70(4): 405-415.

Morell, T. 2004. Interactive lecture discourse for university EFL students. *English for Specific Purposes* 23(3): 325-338.

Morell, T. 2007. What enhances EFL students' participation in lecture discourse? Student, lecturer and discourse perspectives. *Journal of English for Academic Purposes* 6(3): 222-237.

Morley, J. 1995. Academic listening comprehension instruction: Models, principles, and practice. In D. Mendelsohn & J. Rubin (eds.). *A Guide for the Teaching of Second Language Listening*. San Diego: Dominie Press. 186-221.

Muter, V. & K. Diethelm. 2001. The contribution of phonological skills and letter knowledge to early reading development in a multilingual population. *Language Learning* 51(2): 187-219.

Nation, I. S. P. 2006. Second language vocabulary. In K. Brown (ed.). *Encyclopedia of Language and Linguistics* (2nd ed.). Oxford: Elsevier. 448-454.

Nation, I. S. P. 2012. Teaching language in use: Vocabulary. In M. Eisenmann & T. Summer (eds.). *Basic Issues in EFL Teaching and Learning*. Heidelberg: University Winter Verlag. 103-116.

National Communication Association (NCA). 1998. *Competent Communicators: K-12 Speaking, Listening, and Media Literacy Standards and Competency Statements*. Annandale: National Communication Association.

O'Malley, J. M. & A. U. Chamot. 1990. *Learning Strategies in Second Language Acquisition*. Cambridge: Cambridge University Press.

Oatley, K. & J. M. Jenkins. 1996. *Understanding Emotions*. Cambridge, MA: Blackwell.

O'Brien, I., N. Segalowitz, B. Freed & J. Collentine. 2007. Phonological memory predicts second language oral fluency gains in adults. *Studies in Second Language Acquisition* 29(4): 557-581.

Odgers, T. 2009. Leading in international and intercultural education. Presentation presented at Centre for Excellence in Intercultural Education, Norquest College, Edmonton, Albert, Canada.

Paivio, A. 1986. *Mental Representation: A Dual Coding Approach*. Oxford: Oxford University Press.

Paul, R. & L. Elder. 2006. *Critical Thinking: Learn the Tools the Best Thinkers Use*. New Jersey: Pearson Prentice Hall.

Peters, E. & S. Webb. 2018. Incidental vocabulary acquisition through viewing

L2 television and factors that affect learning. *Studies in Second Language Acquisition* 40(3): 551-557.

Peverly, S. T. & J. F. Sumowski. 2012.What variables predict quality of text notes and are text notes related to performance on different types of tests? *Applied Cognitive Psychology* 26(1): 104-117.

Price, K. 1983. Closed-captioned TV: An untapped resource. *MATESOL Newsletter* 12(2): 1-8.

Rahimirad, M. & M. R. Moini. 2015. The challenges of listening to academic lectures for EAP learners and the impact of metacognition on academic lecture listening comprehension. *SAGE Open* 5(2): 1-9.

Richards, J. C. 1983. Listening comprehension: Approach, design, procedure. *TESOL Quarterly* 17(2): 219-240.

Rodgers, M. P. H. & S. Webb. 2020. Incidental vocabulary learning through viewing television. *ITL-International Journal of Applied Linguistics* 171(2): 191-220.

Rost, M. 2002. *Teaching and Researching Listening*. London/New York: Routledge.

Rost, M. 2011. *Teaching and Researching Listening* (2nd ed.). London/New York: Routledge

Rowley-Jolivet, E. 2002. Visual discourse in scientific conference papers: A genre-based study. *English for Specific Purposes* 21(1): 19-40.

Rubin, J. 1994. A review of second language listening comprehension research. *The Modern Language Journal* 78(2): 199-221.

Rubin, J., A. U. Chamot, V. Harris & N. J. Anderson. 2007. Intervening in the use of strategies. In A. Cohen & E. Macaro (eds.). *Language Learner Strategies: Thirty Years of Research and Practice*. Oxford: Oxford University Press. 141-160.

Rumelhart, D. E. 1980. Schemata: The building blocks of cognition. In R. J. Spiro, B. C. Bruce & W. E. Brewer (eds.). *Theoretical Issues in Reading Comprehension*. Hillsdale, NJ: Erlbaum. 33-58.

Sanders, T. J. M. & M. A. Gernsbacher. 2004. Accessibility in text and discourse processing. *Discourse Processes* 37(2): 79-89.

Scarcella, R. & R. W. Rumberger. 2000. Academic English key to long-term success in school. *University of California Linguistic Minority Research Institute Newsletter* 9: 1-2.

Schmidt-Rinehart, B. C. 1994. The effect of topic familiarity on second language listening comprehension. *The Modern Language Journal* 78(2): 179-189.

Schmitt, N. 2008. Instructed second language vocabulary learning. *Language Teaching Research* 12(3): 329-363.

Scriven, M. & R. Paul. 2008. *Defining Critical Thinking.* http://www.criticalthinking. org/aboutCT/define_critical_thinking.cfm (accessed 16/12/2014).

Shannon, C. E. & W. Weaver. 1949. *The Mathematical Theory of Communication.* Urbana, IL: University of Illinois Press.

Siegel, J. 2014. Exploring L2 listening instruction: Examinations of practice. *ELT Journal* 68(1): 22-30.

Smialek, T. & R. Boburka. 2006. The effect of cooperative listening exercises on the critical listening skills of college music-appreciation students. *Journal of Research in Music Education* 54(1): 57-72.

Snow, C. & P. Uccelli. 2009. The challenge of academic language. In D. R. Olson, & N. Torrance (eds.). *The Cambridge Handbook of Literacy.* Cambridge: Cambridge University Press. 112-133.

Stæhr, L. S. 2009. Vocabulary knowledge and advanced listening comprehension in English as a foreign language. *Studies in Second Language Acquisition* 31(4): 577-607.

Thompson, I. & J. Rubin. 1996. Can strategy instruction improve listening comprehension? *Foreign Language Annals* 29(3): 331-342.

Thompson, S. E. 2003. Text-structuring metadiscourse, intonation and the signalling of organisation in academic lectures. *Journal of English for Academic Purposes* 2(1): 5-20.

Tyler, R. W. 1949. *Basic Principles of Curriculum and Instruction.* Chicago: University of Chicago Press.

Van Zeeland, H. & N. Schmitt. 2013. Incidental vocabulary acquisition through L2 listening: A dimensions approach. *System* 41(3): 609-624.

Vandergrift, L. 2006. Second language listening: Listening ability or language proficiency? *The Modern Language Journal* 90(1): 6-18.

Vandergrift, L. 2007. Recent developments in second and foreign language listening comprehension research. *Language Teaching* 40(3): 191-210.

Vandergrift, L., C. C. M. Goh, C. Mareschal & M. Tafaghodtari. 2006. The metacognitive awareness listening questionnaire: Development and validation. *Language Learning* 56(3): 431-462.

Vandergrift, L. & C. C. M. Goh. 2012. *Teaching and Learning Second Language*

Listening: Metacognition in Action. New York: Routledge.

Vandergrift, L. & J. Cross. 2014. Captioned video: How much listening is really going on. *Contact* 40(3): 31-33.

Vandergrift, L. & M. H. Tafaghodtari. 2010. Teaching L2 learners how to listen does make a difference: An empirical study. *Language Learning* 60(2): 470-497.

Vanderplank, R. 1990. Paying attention to the words: Practical and theoretical problems in watching television programmes with uni-lingual (CEEFAX) subtitles. *System* 18(2): 221-234.

Vanderplank, R. 1994. Resolving inherent conflicts: Autonomous language learning from popular broadcast television. In H. Jung & R. Vanderplank (eds.). *Barriers and Bridges: Media Technology in Language Learning*. Frankfurt: Peter Lang. 119-134.

Vanderplank, R. 2010. Déjà vu? A decade of research on language laboratories, television and video in language learning. *Language Teaching* 43(1):1-37.

Warschauer, M., H. Shetzer & C. Meloni. 2000. *Internet for English Teaching*. Alexandria: TESOL.

Webb, S. & M. P. H. Rodgers. 2009a. The lexical coverage of movies. *Applied Linguistics* 30(3): 407-427.

Webb, S. & M. P. H. Rodgers. 2009b. The vocabulary demands of television programs. *Language Learning* 59(2): 335-366.

Webb, S. & P. Nation. 2017. *How Vocabulary is Learned*. Oxford: Oxford University Press.

Weir, C. J. 2003. A survey of the history of the certificate of proficiency in English (CPE) in the twentieth century. In C. J. Weir & M. Milanovic (eds.). *Continuity and Innovation: Revising the Cambridge Proficiency in English Examination 1913-2002*. Cambridge: Cambridge University Press. 1-56.

Wen, Q. F. & R. K. Johnson. 1997. L2 learner variables and English achievement: A study of tertiary-level English majors in China. *Applied Linguistics* 18(1): 27-48.

Wolvin, A. D. & C. G. Coakley. 1994. Listening competency. *International Journal of Listening* 8(1): 148-160.

Wolvin, A. D. & C. G. Coakley. 1996. *Listening* (5th ed.). New York: McGraw Hill.

Wong, P. C. M., E. Skoe, N. M. Russo, N. Dees & N. Kraus. 2007. Musical experience shapes human brainstem encoding of linguistic pitch patterns. *Nature Neuroscience* 10(4): 420-422.

陈琦、高云，2010，学术英语中的半技术性词汇，《外语教学》（6）：42-46。

高永晨，2014，中国大学生跨文化交际能力测评体系的理论框架构建，《外语界》（4）：80-88。

葛春萍、王守仁，2016，跨文化交际能力培养与大学英语教学，《外语与外语教学》（2）：79-86+146。

关世杰，1995，《跨文化交流学》。北京：北京大学出版社。

胡文仲，2013，跨文化交际能力在外语教学中如何定位，《外语界》（6）：2-8。

胡文仲，2018，外语教育改革二三事，《外语界》（4）：2-7。

黄源深，1998，思辨缺席，《外语与外语教学》（7）：1+19。

教育部高等学校大学外语教学指导委员会，2020，《大学英语教学指南（2020版)》。北京：高等教育出版社。

教育部高等学校教学指导委员会（编），2018，《普通高等学校本科专业类教学质量国家标准》。北京：高等教育出版社。

教育部、国家语言文字工作委员会，2018，《中国英语能力等级量表》。北京：高等教育出版社。

勒博布（Lebauber, R. S.）著，卢小萍、姜蓉译，2006，《朗文英语讲座听力：学生用书》。北京：北京语言大学出版社。

刘思，1995，英语听力词汇量与阅读词汇量——词汇研究调查报告，《外语教学与研究》（1）：61-65。

满蓉、王劲，2011，英文歌曲应用于大一新生语音教学的探讨，《外国语文》（S1）：94-96。

欧洲理事会文化合作教育委员会，刘骏、傅荣等译，2008，《欧洲语言共同参考框架：学习、教学、评估》。北京：外语教学与研究出版社。

沈渭菊，2011，电影教学在大学英语教学中的作用之实证研究，《电化教育研究》（3）：106-112。

孙有中，2011，突出思辨能力培养，将英语专业教学改革引向深入，《中国外语》（3）：49-58.

孙有中，2016，外语教育与跨文化能力培养，《中国外语》（3）：1+17-22。

孙有中，2017，人文英语教育论，《外语教学与研究》（6）：859-870。

孙有中等，2011，英语专业写作教学与思辨能力培养座谈，《外语教学与研究》（4）：603-608。

汪清，2011，意义协商中的语言输出研究，《外语与外语教学》（2）：43-47。

王红，2000，听歌法在英语听说课上的有效应用，《国外外语教学》（4）：40-41+32。

王秋云，2015，英语歌曲辅助 EFL 学习之回顾与展望，《西安外国语大学学报》
　　（4）：78-81。

王艳，2012，《英语听力教学与研究》。北京：外语教学与研究出版社。

王艳，2014，《中国大学生二语听力理解能力模型构建》。北京：外语教学与研
　　究出版社。

王艳，2015，思辨听力：理据、框架与操作，《中国外语》（2）：80-85。

王艳，2018，以语言能力、思辨能力和跨文化能力为目标构建外语听力教学新
　　模式，《外语教学》（6）：69-73。

王艳，2019，思辨听力课堂的同伴互动研究，《外语教育研究前沿》（2）：25-
　　32。

文秋芳，1999，《英语口语测试与教学》。上海：上海外语教育出版社。

文秋芳，2016，在英语通用语背景下重新认识语言与文化的关系，《外语教学
　　理论与实践》（2）：1-7+13。

文秋芳、孙旻，2015，评述高校外语教学中思辨力培养存在的问题，《外语教
　　学理论与实践》（3）：6-12+94。

文秋芳、王海妹、王建卿、赵彩然、刘艳萍，2010，我国英语专业与其他文科
　　类大学生思辨能力的对比研究，《外语教学与研究》（5）：350-355+400。

文秋芳、王建卿、赵彩然、刘艳萍、王海妹，2009，构建我国外语类大学生思
　　辨能力量具的理论框架，《外语界》（1）：37-43。

文秋芳、周燕，2006，评述外语专业学生思维能力的发展，《外语学刊》（5）：
　　76-80。

杨亚丽、杨帆，2014，以学术英语为导向的研究生英语课程设置模式，《高等
　　农业教育》（8）：86-89。

赵炬明，2018，聚焦设计：实践与方法（上）——美国"以学生为中心"的本
　　科教学改革研究之三，《高等教育工程》（3）：29-44。

郑仲华，1989，学术听力教学中心理语言学的应用，《外语界》（4）：7-11。

钟兰凤、钟家宝，2015，研究生学术英语焦虑现状及影响因素研究，《外语研
　　究》（6）：56-61+112。

庄恩平，2006，跨文化能力：我国 21 世纪人才必备的能力——"2006 跨文化
　　交际国际学术研讨会"综述，《外语界》（5）：79-80。